BOUNDLESS
COOKBOOK

BEN GREENFIELD

CONTENTS

6 INTRODUCTION

12 01 STEAK
16 Ben's Sous Vide Steak
20 Reverse Sear Steak
24 Ben's "Boiled Steak"

27 02 STEAK RUBS
28 Black Salt Rub
28 Rub-With-A-Kick
29 Coffee Rub

30 03 FISH
32 Salmon Cakes
34 Lazy Man's Sushi Hand Roll
36 Sous Vide Salmon
39 Spam Musubi

43 04 WILD GAME
45 Axis Rib Roast
48 Braised Boar Belly
50 Mutton Leg Roast

53 05 ORGAN MEAT
55 Liver and Onions
59 "Nature's Multivitamin" Breakfast Burrito
60 Perfectly Scrambled Eggs

62 06 CHICKEN
64 Beer Can Chicken
67 Jessa's World-Famous Roasted Chicken

70	**07**	**BREAD**
72		Low-Carb High-Collagen Chocolate Nut Butter Loaf
74		Dr. Sarah Myhill's Linseed Loaf
77		Jessa Greenfield's World-Famous Sourdough Bread
81		Sourdough Bread Pizza
83	**08**	**VEGETABLES**
84		Sweet Potato Fries
86		Carrot Fries
89		Fermented Wild Plant Pesto
93		Sprouts Snack Mix
95	**09**	**SMOOTHIES**
96		The Ultimate Anti-Aging Morning Smoothie
100		Avocado Chocolate Pudding
102		Pumpkin Pie Smoothie
104		Carrot Cake Açaí Bowl
106		Elemental Diet Smoothie
108		Go Greenfields Banana Spiced Oatless Oatmeal
110	**10**	**COFFEE AND TEA**
112		Cacao-Chaga Sipping Chocolate
114		Reishi Relaxation Tea
114		Black Pepper Tea
115		Nighttime Autophagy Tea
116	**11**	**BROTHS**
118		Dr. Thomas Cowan's Bone Broth Breakfast
120		Ben's Thanksgiving Leftovers Bone Broth Kitchen Sink Recipe
123	**12**	**FERMENTS**
125		Creamy, Creamy Kefir
128		Collagen Coconut Yogurt
131		Immortality Yogurt
134		Bedtime Jello

136   **13**   DESSERT

137   Barùkas Nut Cheesecake
140   Barùkas Chocolate-Vanilla Nut Butter
142   Paleo Pumpkin Donuts
144   Pumpkin Custard
146   Gut-Healing Keto Ice Cream
146   Peanut-Butter-Chocolate Keto Ice Cream
146   Screamin' Sex Ice Cream
150   Zero-Carb Japanese "Jelly Cubes"
153   Sourdough Cinnamon Rolls

155   **14**   COCKTAILS

159   Ben & Jitters
161   Elderberry Juice and Organic Wine Over Ice
162   Moscow Mule with Zevia Ginger Beer

164   **15**   RESOURCES

164   Books
165   Kitchen Tools, Materials, and Equipment
165   Meat, Fish, and Chicken
166   Pantry items
167   Supplements
168   Websites

169   **16**   REFERENCES

171   **17**   ABOUT THE AUTHOR

174   **18**   FINAL WORDS

INTRODUCTION

I'm not a chef.

Yes, I'm definitely *not* a chef. With zero formal training in cooking, I've achieved any remote semblance of cooking chops I might have via learning recipes from a mash-up of cooking videos I've come across on YouTube (e.g. random Google searches for terms like, "How to make liver taste good"), listening to simple tips my wife mutters as she passes by me in the kitchen while I attempt to make myself a proper meal (e.g. "Babe, add a bit of coconut flour to those salmon cakes, and they'll stop crumbling on you!"), and reading insightful tips and tricks from the host of nutrition and cookbooks I read and review on a weekly basis (e.g. mix lemon juice with your bone broth to increase collagen bioavailability).

Sure, I took advanced courses in biochemistry, chemistry, microbiology, physics, and nutrition in college, and I'm sure those have assisted my learning curve in the kitchen quite dramatically. But, I will be the first to admit that when it comes to cooking, and especially writing a cookbook, I have full-blown imposter syndrome. My wife? She's a rancher girl who can, with nary a drop of sweat, whip up a crispy roasted chicken on a Friday night and a batch of mouth-watering sourdough cinnamon rolls on a Saturday morning, all from scratch. My twin boys? They've been taking cooking classes since they were four years old and can expertly fashion a chocolate souffle and mushroom risotto for their freaking lunch. Me? I grew up on boxed macaroni and cheese, 29 cent hamburgers, frozen hot dogs, and whey protein shakes. So for most of my life, I was pretty much limited to a microwave, a blender, and a drive-thru.

Yet, I do like to tinker in the kitchen. I thoroughly enjoy cracking the code on how to use science and spices to unlock nutrients and enhance the digestibility of the vast array of scrumptious foods we're blessed with on this planet. And heck, as a self-proclaimed foodie, I *definitely* like to eat and furthermore like to eat *good food*. So as a result of my passion for all things food and health, I'm asked with surprising and increased frequency for all the crazy and unique recipes I frequently mention on podcasts and articles or feature in so-called "food porn" photos on social media.

So I finally decided to sit down and churn out a cookbook chock-full of my favorite recipes — recipes that are mentioned, often with great scientific detail, in my book *Boundless* and across my media platforms — but recipes that have never been fully fleshed out in terms of exact ingredients and preparation strategies. In other words, it's one thing to read in *Boundless* about how fermenting your own yogurt changes the biome of the gut in a favorable manner and enhances many aspects of endocrine and immune function. But it's quite another matter to know exactly how I wake up in the morning and quickly whip up a batch of homemade yogurt; the specific strains of bacteria I use; the methods I use to make those bacteria more concentrated or bioavailable; what I mix with the yogurt for goals such as sleep enhancement or muscle building, or even how long the darn stuff stays good in the refrigerator.

Ultimately, you can consider this *Boundless Cookbook* to be my own personal collection of recipes for boundless energy — recipes that are woven into my daily and weekly routine as true dietary staples. (Yep, I regularly eat *everything* in this cookbook.) And, you can also consider this cookbook to be the perfect companion to the book, *Boundless*.

Lest my own hair-brained recipes be a bit too strange for you, I've also woven in several of my wife's most popular, most-asked-for recipes such as her famous roast chicken, her incredible sourdough bread, and her mouth-watering sourdough cinnamon rolls, as well as a few of the wildly creative recipes that have emerged from my twin sons' Go Greenfields (GoGreenfields. com) cooking website and podcast.

But before diving into the actual recipes, I'd like to give you a few tips that have significantly enhanced my own relationship with food, diet, and nutrition.

First, as you begin your own tinkering in the kitchen with these recipes and start to explore the collection of new foods or ingredients you'll find within the pages of this cookbook, I encourage you to **prepare your food mindfully**.

Take a simple cup of coffee, for example. Sure, you can rush to your kitchen in the morning, curse as you fumble with the coffee filter, quickly prepare your water as you glance at your watch and think about your email inbox, then hover over your coffee, sipping madly as you scroll through text messages. Alternatively, you can slowly open the bag of coffee, take a satisfying whiff of the intense aroma of floral and cacao, perk up your ears as you listen to the whooshing and light sprinkling of the water as it falls into the kettle or coffee maker, and take those first few sips with your eyes closed, fully mindful and grateful of a rich superfood from South America that has magically appeared in your kitchen to fire up your precious brain for a day of impactful and purposeful work. *See the difference?* **Food and drink should be enjoyed with the full array of senses, prepared, and consumed mindfully and gratefully.**

Truly, in our tiny pantries and humble kitchens, we now have access to the same cinnamons and spices from the Orient, fruits and beans from the Amazon, and the dried berries and cured meats and cheeses from Northern Europe that kings and queens of old would have paid buckets of gold for and sent out explorers, sailors, and armies on quests to collect.

As you approach food in a more mindful way, you may (especially if you like music or play a musical instrument) enjoy thinking of preparing and eating food a bit like making music, which is a practice that requires a great deal of mindfulness. Managing multiple pans on the stove can be like playing the drums and finely slicing a clove of garlic like tuning a mandolin. Would you play the drums with a phone cradled to your ear or tune a violin while sending a text message? Approach food preparation, and even food consumption, similarly.

Second, I encourage you to **be in constant awe at the wonders of God's creation**. I'm ceaselessly aware of the magic, beauty, mystery, and wonder of the vast array of superfoods scattered across this Earth. Take a variant of the humble buckwheat plant, for example, the Himalayan Tartary Buckwheat, which I made blueberry pancakes with last Saturday morning as a surprise for my boys (served alongside the Perfect Scrambled Eggs recipe you'll find in this cookbook).

Himalayan Tartary Buckwheat (let's call it HTB so as not to get too long in the tooth) is a hardy plant that has been farmed in Asia for generations but is largely unknown in the rest of the world. Modern analyses have revealed that HTB (BigBoldHealth.com/news/the-story-of-big-bold-health/) contains significantly higher levels of phytonutrients compared to common buckwheat — up to a 100-fold increase of certain immune-strengthening flavonoids. HTB is also incredibly rich in the flavonoids rutin, quercetin, hesperidin, luteolin, and diosmin. Nutritionally speaking, this portfolio of flavonoids is an orchestra, a symphony, and a masterpiece of the Creator's genius. Each is unique, but together they are wondrous, especially when it comes to the positive ways they can influence immune function.

Next, 2-hydroxybenzylamine (2-HOBA) is a plant chemical that is extremely rare to find in any foods, but it just so happens that HTB is one of the best sources currently known. This chemical, 2-HOBA, is now being studied for how well it stops the formation of many harmful molecules in the body. Calcium-hydroxy-methyl butyrate monohydrate (yep, that's a mouthful) is another significant component of HTB. This nutrient, which is found in alfalfa and other foods, has been studied for immune support and rejuvenation, as well as the ways it helps build, maintain, and protect muscles and lean tissues throughout the body.

Then there's chlorophyllin, also found in high amounts in HTB. In plants, chlorophyll turns light into energy. What can it do for humans? It turns out that it can improve the way the body deals with certain toxins and gets rid of them. At sufficient levels, chlorophyll can protect DNA and chromosomes, and even help cells repair themselves from damage. Heck, if you read a book like Sayer Ji's *Regenerate* or Arturo Herrera's *The Human Photosynthesis*, you'll discover how photons of energy from sunlight can actually interact with the chlorophyll in your bloodstream to generate electrons that allow for the production of cellular energy — even in the absence of calories from food!

Just think about it: that's all from one tiny humble buckwheat plant that has been treasured in Asia for thousands of years but that we, in the West, barely know anything about. (Though we've certainly cracked the code on how to genetically modify wheat and spray it with herbicides and pesticides to make a relatively nutrient-void Frankenplant for our hamburger buns!)

Multitudes of other examples abound that display the mysteries and wonders of superfoods in Creation. From Goji berries and coffeeberry fruit to spirulina and chlorella algae to Barùkas nuts and chia seeds, we walk a planet rich in bountiful blessings. Yet how often do we drop our jaws in pure awe at these mysterious, wonderful fruits of the Earth? In the Bible, Psalm 104:24-25, sums things up quite nicely:

"O Lord, how manifold are Your works!

In wisdom You have made them all.

The earth is full of Your possessions —

This great and wide sea,

In which are innumerable teeming things,

Living things both small and great."

Elsewhere, in John 1:3, we learn that: "All things were through Him; and without Him nothing was made that was made." So yes, that means that Almighty God formed and fashioned the cacao tree, the cannabis plant, the chickpea, and the catfish — and all this marvelous bounty is ours to enjoy in all of its intricacy, beauty and, yes, tastiness.

Next, I urge you — especially if you are religious or immersed in the spiritual disciplines — to **consider food not as just a collection of physical atoms and molecules largely disconnected from the ethereal dimensions of your spirit, but rather as a means to fuel your soul.** The care of your physical body, whether via diet or exercise, can simply be a manifestation of your spirituality. In the book *Living By Design*, authors Ray Strand and Bill Ewing consider health in the light of eternity, emphasizing that good health, including that obtained from eating nourishing, healthy food, brings us closer to God and should be viewed as fuel for fully manifesting our purpose in life.

They say: *"Having a healthy body is not a worthy goal in and of itself. In fact, if we seek that first, we have missed the entire point of our existence. We are called to something infinitely greater and eternally more important: a vibrant relationship with God that overflows into loving service to others and continual worship of Him as our Creator. The body is simply an earthly tool He has loaned us for that purpose. That truth must always come first. Then (if we are wise) we will seek to make that tool as efficient and effective as it can be for that purpose."*

My friend, Dr. Joseph Mercola, speaks similarly when he says: *"If you take care of your body not only do you prevent disease and illness and prolong your life, but you also vastly improve the quality of your life. You can increase your daily energy, creativity, attention span, and mental focus, allowing you to achieve more in the pursuit of whatever matters to you... It only takes common sense to understand that what you put in your body several times a day, every day, will have far more impact on your being than anything else you do."*

In other words, **what you put into your body is not only important for your physical health, but also for your spiritual health and, ultimately, for fulfilling your life's purpose.** For a deeper exploration of this concept, and other compelling thoughts about the intimate link between food and spirituality, I highly recommend the book *Health For Godly Generations* by Renee DeGroot.

Finally, I encourage you to **enjoy your food in a parasympathetic state of relaxation, mindfulness, and gratefulness.** Quickly sucking down your smoothie while hunched over a steering wheel as you stressfully navigate on your morning commute, wiping breakfast shards off your face while fumbling with the music dial on the car is a far, far different experience — both psychologically and physiologically — compared to sitting at your kitchen table in the sunshine, savoring every bite, and perhaps jotting down a few notes in your gratitude journal, thumbing through your favorite magazine or chatting with your family.

Eating in a stressed state predisposes you to leaky gut syndrome, inadequate digestive enzyme production, poor nutrient absorption, and overeating — all topics I explore in great detail in the "How To Fix Your Gut" chapter of my book *Boundless*. In contrast, eating in a relaxed state, often with friends and family, usually in between and not during bouts of work, allows you to savor and enjoy your food, digest your food, and feel more satiated from each and every bite that you mindfully chew. By the way, research has shown that to truly digest your meal, get the maximum nutritional benefit from the food and the minimum inflammatory impact on the gut, an average number of 25-40 times per bite is what you should aim for when chewing your food (you learn plenty more tips about oral care, jaw strength, and how to breathe/chew properly in the "Supermodel: Maximize Your Symmetry and Beauty" chapter of my book *Boundless*). This savoring and gratefulness for food can ultimately bring us closer to our Creator.

So as trite as a bite of truffle may seem, or a post-workout dinner of steak and fries, or an energy drink we might suck down during a triathlon, any pursuit of diet or fitness can bring us closer to our greatest purpose in life if we approach it with the right mentality — by using it to fuel our hearts with the joy and love of God, as Paul so eloquently states in his letter to the Corinthians in the Bible: "Therefore, whether you eat or drink, or whatever you do, do all to the glory of God (1 Cor 10:31)."

John Piper also sums this up quite nicely in Chapter 2 of his excellent book *Don't Waste Your Life* when he says, "*God created you and me to live with a single all-embracing, all-transforming passion — namely a passion to glorify God by enjoying and displaying his supreme excellence in all the spheres of life.*" And yes, that supreme excellence in all spheres of life includes swinging a kettlebell and making a superfood smoothie.

In my own personal experience, I've found that one of the best ways to approach each meal with this spirit of mindfulness, gratitude, and relaxation is to create some kind of routine or ritual for each meal. This pre-meal habit can include a few relaxing breaths, a blessing, a prayer, or even a song. For example, one easy breathwork practice we often implement at the Greenfield dinner table is to simply close the eyes, take a deep, slow breath in through the nose, then out through slightly pursed lips and repeat three times.

Another simple habit is to think of one thing you're grateful for and say it aloud prior to your meal. Or if you are in a group, you can go around the table and have each person name one thing they are grateful for. Or you can say a simple prayer and bless the food. In addition to thanking God for providing yet another blessing of nutrients, calories, and sustenance, I also like this pleasant twist on a Thich Nhat Hanh blessing, which I learned from an attendee at an immersive health event where I teach, called RUNGA. It goes like this:

> *Breathing in, I'm aware of my body.*
> *Breathing out, I smile at my body.*
> *Breathing in, I am aware of my food.*
> *Breathing out, I smile at my food.*
> *Breathing in, I'm aware of my company.*
> *Breathing out, I smile at my company.*

An entire group can easily chant these wonderful words together, eyes closed, breathing in and out together as one person leads and the others repeat the words that person recites.

Does all this seem to make it sound to you like there's a deep spiritual aspect to food? You would be correct if you suspected so. After all, food isn't just about minerals, vitamins, proteins, carbohydrates, fat, and calories. **Food connects us.** Food fuels traditions and memories. Food is something we gather around. Food changes our mood, for better or worse. Food can create bliss and contentment that one feels far beyond their stomach, small intestine, large intestine, and bloodstream. Do not underestimate the invisible energy and frequency contained within each bite that you eat, and the impact of your own energy and frequency on each bite you eat. Food can feed the soul.

So, when the Greenfield family finishes a hard day jam-packed with work, chores, school, phone calls, consults, meetings, emails, workouts, animal care, podcasts, articles, books, and we all finally gather around the dining room table to breathe in the sweet aroma of a salted, roasted chicken with baked carrot fries and fresh sprouts drenched in extra virgin olive oil and dressed with crumbled goat cheese, and I take that first sip of dark, rich organic wine, a smile erupts on my face and also in my soul — not only because of the deep, intense sense of relaxation and pleasure I derive from gathering around a beautiful cornucopia of aromatic food with my precious family, but also because I know I helped grow those sprouts from tiny alfalfa, red clover, and broccoli seeds, and had a chance to participate in the magic of growing, nourishing, and savoring God's creation. I feel blessed to be able to now share some of that goodness with you.

Bon appetit!

Ben Greenfield

P.S. Handy links for all the books, podcasts, cooking tools, ingredients, and anything else mentioned for every recipe in this book can be found on **page 164**.

01

STEAK

Before I reveal my most popular, mouth-watering, tried-and-true steak recipes, it's important that you understand two important things:

1. **The source of your meat is very, very important — in essence, you are "what you eat."**

2. **Red meat, sourced properly, cooked intelligently, consumed in moderation and combined with the right nutrients, is not going to cause you to die an early, horrible death of cancer or heart disease.**

Let's begin with point #1 above. A big thanks to my friend Evgeny Trufkin, author of the handy *Anti-Factory Farm Shopping Guide* for elucidating this issue in detail in his book, which I highly recommend you grab and devour if you are going to eat anything you haven't grown or hunted yourself.

Say it takes like 18 months to raise cattle from start to finish. Ninety-eight percent of cattle are raised the bulk majority of their life on pasture, being fed grass. However, 3-4 months before harvest, nearly every cow is sent to a feedlot where it is then grain-finished. Finishing the cattle on grain increases the omega-6 fatty acid content, which can contribute to inflammation. (If you want to delve more deeply into a host of other problematic issues, such as hormones, antibiotics, unethical treatment of animals, poor regenerative farming practices, etc., then read my book *Boundless*, or Evgeny's book cited above.)

But what about grass-fed, grass-finished beef? Fact is, farmers are allowed to raise their cattle on grass for 8-10 months, then transition them to grains for 3-4 months, and finish them on grass for 1 week — yet still throw the grass-fed, grass-finished label on there.

So where can you get high-quality meat these days that satisfies the criteria of grass-fed, grass-finished, grown in a regenerative, sustainable, ethical manner?

Evgeny recommends opting for local grass-fed operations. Check out the **American Grassfed Association** (AmericanGrassfed.com). Scroll to the bottom of the site, and click on the map. Then select your state and you'll find what you're looking for.

A few of my other favorite sources include:

- *Thrive Market:* 100% grass-fed, pasture-raised beef shipped right to your door. All of their beef comes from Osorno, Chile, where grass is abundant and the climate is ideal for letting cows graze outdoors year-round. No chemicals, artificial fertilizers, or antibiotics are used. Low-density grazing methods are used to maintain the integrity of the precious land and soil.

- *BelCampo Meats:* Pasture-raised beef, pork, poultry, lamb, and more from certified-organic, humane farms using regenerative practices.

- *US Wellness Meats:* Tender and tasty, without all the excess fat of animals fed with grain in confinement. Full of nutrients that can only come from a fully grass-fed diet — omega-3 fatty acids, vitamin A, vitamin E, and CLA — and free of all the pesticides, hormones, and antibiotics that are found in grain-fed beef.

- *White Oak Pastures:* Grass-fed beef, goat, and lamb and pastured chicken, duck, goose, and more. Animals are raised in a regenerative manner using humane animal management practices.

- *Eat Wild:* The #1 clearinghouse for information about pasture-based farming that features a state-by-state plus Canada directory of local farmers who sell their pastured farm and ranch products directly to consumers.

- *Piedmontese Beef:* The Piedmontese is a breed of domestic cattle that originated in the region of Piedmont, in north-west Italy. It has higher protein per ounce than beef from other breeds, and the steaks, in particular, all grass-fed and grass-finished, tend to be quite tender and full of flavor.

Next, regarding point #2 above, yes: it's true — red meat is not going to kill you. In his book, *The Carnivore Code*, my friend Paul Saladino summed it up quite nicely when I asked him to explain this to my readers:

"Most of the misconceptions that red meat causes cancer comes from a report by the World Health Organization's International Agency for Research on Cancer (IARC) that was released in 2015. Sounds like a really fancy title, doesn't it? Surely, something coming out of an organization like that would be reliable and reputable, right? Sadly, this report has been wildly misinterpreted by mainstream media and is based on some very questionable interpretations of the science it claims to review.

"Of the fourteen epidemiology studies that were included in the IARC report, eight showed no link between the consumption of meat and the development of colon cancer. Yes, you read that correctly, the

majority of the studies considered in this report did not show a correlation between the consumption of red meat and colon cancer. Of the remaining six studies, only one showed a statistically significant correlation between meat and cancer.

"Thus, in the IARC report, only one of the fourteen studies considered showed a correlation between red meat and cancer that achieved statistical significance. This is what we are basing wide-sweeping recommendations on? What about the other 13 that did not show any associations or in which statistical significance was not reached? Furthermore, looking at the data considered by the IARC report, it's also clear that all of the interventional studies in animals, which also do not show a connection between red meat and cancer, were left out of consideration.

"With red meat and lifespan, the story is the same. These claims are based on little more than very misleading and poorly done epidemiology and there are studies that suggest the complete opposite, showing an association between consumption of red meat and longer telomeres.

"What about heart disease? This is a deep rabbit hole, but the cliff notes version is that in the setting of metabolic health, and insulin sensitivity, it's nearly impossible to make the case that LDL (which may rise slightly with increased saturated fat consumption) or cholesterol are the real culprits in the formation of atherosclerotic plaque formation or progression. There's also a large amount of evidence to the contrary, showing strong correlations in those greater than 65 years old between higher levels of LDL and longevity as well as resilience against infectious illnesses. Contrary to popular belief, more LDL is probably a good thing if you are healthy overall, and saturated fat from well-raised animals is a very healthy part of the human diet, and always has been.

"At the most basic, intuitive level, let's also consider the fact that humans have been eating red meat and organs from ruminant animals for millions of years, and that this was probably the single greatest factor in our evolution that allowed our brains to grow — turning us into the incredibly resourceful species we are today. Why would such foods be bad for us? Wouldn't such an environmental/genetic mismatch have been selected out of our gene pool long ago?

"When it comes to animal meat and organs, quality certainly matters, both from an environmental and nutritional standpoint. But if we are eating regeneratively raised, grass-fed, grass-finished animals, we are eating in a way that is consistent with thousands of generations of our ancestors before us and with the current living indigenous groups who enjoy robust health and freedom from the chronic diseases that plague our modernized Western culture. We should not be misled by frequently misinterpreted epidemiology, and we should not be afraid of eating in such evolutionarily consistent ways. Instead, we should embrace well-raised animal foods as unparalleled sources of nutrition and make them the centerpiece of our diet."

For more, read Paul's book *The Carnivore Code*. I'm not a strict carnivore guy myself, but it's an excellent read nonetheless. Ultimately, the takeaway message is that you're not going to get cancer or heart disease from a properly-comprised diet that includes a "nose-to-tail" approach to animal consumption from healthy animals (to truly obtain all of the nutrients you need to thrive, organs like liver, bone marrow, spleen, heart, kidney, thymus, intestines, and testicle are crucial, as you'll learn later in this cookbook.)

Alright, testicles aside, I'd say that's a hefty enough intro to the steak section, don't you think? With a consideration not to over-consume red meat because, as I explain in detail in my book *Boundless*, some amount of red meat and protein restriction can be favorable for longevity, I personally have a nice cut of steak 2-3 times per week, so let's dive into a few of my favorite steak recipes.

For all resources, books, tools, and ingredients mentioned throughout this chapter go to:
BoundlessCookbook.com/steak

BEN'S SOUS VIDE STEAK

Sous vide cooking is simply the process of sealing food in an airtight container — usually a sealed bag — and then cooking that food in water that is temperature-controlled. Chefs, in many top restaurants around the world, use this tactic to get a very consistent, perfect cook on meat by vacuum sealing a protein with marinade, sauce, herbs, or spices and then dropping it in a large pot of water.

A sous vide machine typically uses a heated metal coil to warm water to a constant temperature that never fluctuates to high or low extremes. This means that the cooking progress is gradual and controlled. Since the water never goes past the desired temperature of doneness, the meat takes a bit longer to cook (a proper sous vide steak can take a couple of hours). But it also means that you'll never have an overcooked piece of protein, and there's not a lot of maintenance: you just put your meat, herbs, marinade, etc. into the bag, drop the bag into the water, set your timer, and walk away. I personally use a Joule brand sous vide wand, which syncs to my phone and can send me an alert when my recipe is ready, which is quite convenient.

One common concern about sous vide is the potential for plastic leaching into the food. For this reason, I use silicone Stasher bags. This brand not only helps the planet (you can reuse them over and over again, unlike single-use plastics) but importantly, each bag is made of pure platinum food-grade silicone that is much safer to cook in if you are concerned about plastics in your food (which you should be). You can sous vide multiple steaks at a time, but I recommend just one steak per sous vide bag.

Finally, the blueberries are a fantastic addition to this recipe. Why? Turns out an impressive study shows that combining a nutrient found in beef (carnosine) with blueberries can send your energy levels skyrocketing. It does this by supercharging your stem cells more than 80%! Wow! The added bonus is that the sweet tartness of the blueberries pairs amazingly with the rich, salty flavor of the sous vide beef.

Total Time

80 minutes

Tools And Materials

Sous vide wand

Silicone Stasher bags

Ingredients

A thick, juicy steak*

Extra virgin olive oil
(about 2 tablespoons per steak)

Any good salt, to taste (about 1 teaspoon)

Black pepper, to taste (about 1 teaspoon)

Cayenne pepper, to taste
(about 1 teaspoon)

2 minced garlic cloves per steak

A sprig of rosemary and/or thyme per steak

Tarragon or dill, to taste
(about 1 teaspoon)

Half a dozen to a dozen blueberries per steak (optional)

Butter, about 2 tablespoons give or take

*Notes

For the steak, I tend to be partial to a big ol' bone-in ribeye from US Wellness Meats or Bel Campo.

Instructions

1. Sear the steak in 1 tablespoon extra virgin olive oil on a hot cast iron skillet for 1 minute each side. This step is optional but will help to "lock-in" flavor before the sous vide step.
2. Put the steak into a bag with another tablespoon of extra virgin olive oil, and then add all the spices, garlic, rosemary and/or thyme, tarragon and/or dill, and blueberries. Shake the bag vigorously for 30 seconds to mix everything, then seal the bag well.
3. Sous vide the steak for 75-90 minutes. (This will depend on steak thickness. Most sous vide systems include instructions for ideal temperature and time.) I have found a sweet spot of 75 minutes at 129 °F.
4. After finishing the sous vide, remove the steaks from the bags and transfer them onto a hot skillet. Sear for 90 seconds each side to get a perfect crunchy outer coating and tender, evenly cooked middle (it will be about medium-rare).
5. If you like, after searing the steak, you can dump the entire contents of the bag (spices, herbs, blueberries, and oil) onto the skillet, and simmer down for 2-3 minutes to create a dipping sauce for your steak. When I do this, I often add a bit of butter for an even thicker, more flavorful sauce. A real kitchen whiz can even get this sauce going as the steaks are quickly searing and use the butter blueberry sauce to baste the steaks while they're cooking. You get bonus points and a bonus for your taste buds if you decide to pull that off!

REVERSE SEAR
STEAK

Using a reverse sear steak method will allow for more odds of cooking the perfect steak while maximizing flavor. You simply cook the meat at a low temperature in the oven first and then sear it at the very end. I find I get a much more predictable, flavorful, and even cook when using this method.

For this particular recipe, I highly recommend the Black Coffee Rub that's under Steak Rubs (page 27) in this cookbook. The antioxidants in the coffee rub will naturally lower any carcinogens from cooking the meat. And, the mix of the avocado oil with the coarse, crunchy, moist coffee-salt rub enhances every bite of this steak with an explosion of crunchy, salty goodness.

Total Time

30 minutes

Tools And Materials

Meat thermometer

Wire rack that fits over a large
baking sheet

Ingredients

Steak, 1 thick-cut*

Rub of choice (I highly recommend
the black coffee rub), enough to
season both sides of the steak

Extra virgin olive oil or clarified butter
like ghee or avocado oil (optional),
about a tablespoon or so

Chopped fresh rosemary, a sprig or two

Chopped fresh thyme, a sprig or two

*Notes

Cooking a steak using this method is best for thicker cuts, typically a minimum of
1½-inch to 2-inch thick (anything below tends to cook too quickly). Try to choose a
cut with a significant amount of visible marbling, such as ribeye, top sirloin, New York
strip, porterhouse, or filet mignon.

Instructions

1. Preheat the oven to 275 °F.
2. Place a large cast iron skillet in the oven to preheat. This kickstarts the cooking
   process and speeds up the time it takes to sear the steak.
3. Place a wire rack on top of a large baking sheet.
4. Dry the surface of the steak with paper towels to remove excess moisture.
5. Place the steak on the wire rack, and season both sides with coffee rub.

Cook The Steak In The Oven First

While cooking the steak in the oven, use a meat thermometer to monitor the internal temperature of the thickest part of the steak. Usually, after about 15 minutes, you'll be getting close to 90-95 °F for medium-rare or after a few more minutes 100-105 °F for medium. (The steaks are going to keep cooking, so don't worry if this seems like too low a temperature.)

Pan Sear The Steak

1. Remember that cast iron skillet you heated in the oven? Now is the time to remove it, and transfer it to the stovetop.
2. Turn the stovetop heat to high. Then, once the pan is hot, add an oil that has a high smoke point temperature. I like to use extra virgin olive oil or clarified butter like ghee. You can also use avocado oil. Sprinkle the fresh rosemary and thyme around the oil in the pan and also on top of the steak.
3. Sear the steak on each side for about 2 minutes, or until the desired doneness or internal temperature is reached. (Aim for an internal temperature of 120-125 °F for medium-rare or 130 °F for medium.)
4. An option is to add the butter toward the end of cooking to the pan, beside the steak. Spoon the hot melted butter on top to baste the steaks for enhanced browning and flavor.
5. If your steak is thick, as it should be, finish by quickly searing the sides of the steak to render the fat, about 30-60 seconds per side.
6. Finally, remove the steak from the skillet to a clean plate or a separate wire rack set on a baking sheet. Allow to rest for 5-10 minutes, then eat!

BEN'S "BOILED STEAK"

Even though it sounds strange, I discovered that you can actually make quite a flavorful steak without any oil, any mess, and minimal clean up with just a bit of boiling water and a cold water bath.

When creating this recipe, my goal was to kill any bacteria on the surface of the meat, while still having the ability to eat the meat somewhat raw, which I actually enjoy for a change in flavor and a bit more of a primal, caveman feel.

Granted, this recipe doesn't allow for a crunchy outer sear to your steak, so think of it more like tartare or carpaccio. Some have criticized me for simply "boiling" a steak, but... don't knock it till you've tried it! Once you try this method and smother the steak afterward with a good healthy mayonnaise (I like the Primal Kitchen Aioli Mayo but any of their varieties will do) and/or sprinkle a bit of goat cheese on top along with a selection of your favorite spices, it tastes amazing, especially when thin-sliced carpaccio style with a super sharp steak knife.

Total Time

5 minutes

Tools And Materials

Kitchen tongs

Ingredients

Steak, 1 bone-in ribeye*

A pot of boiling water

Another pot of cold water + a few handfuls of ice

A healthy, non-vegetable oil mayonnaise, 1-2 tablespoons

Goat cheese (optional), about a tablespoon, crumbled

Your favorite selection of spices or any of the rubs from this cookbook, about 1-2 tablespoons

*Notes

I usually use a large French ribeye (about 1.5 lbs,1-1.5 inches thick) from US Wellness Meats.

Instructions

1. Heat a large pot of water to boiling temperature. Drop your steak into the boiling water, and leave it there for about 3-4 minutes. While it's there, fill another pot with water and a few handfuls of ice.

2. After 3-4 minutes, use a pair of kitchen tongs to fetch the steak from the boiling water, then drop it into the ice water for about 1 minute. (This step seems to give the steak a nice, firm texture.)

3. Remove from the ice water, pat dry, then smother with mayonnaise, goat cheese, any of your favorite spices, rubs, or herbs, and then enjoy thin-sliced carpaccio style. This is quite a unique and flavorful experience, with minimal preparation or cleanup.

STEAK RUBS

There's nothing like a well-formulated steak rub to blast the flavor of a good cut of meat through the roof, and also reduce potential carcinogens that can accumulate on meat during high-heat cooking, grilling, or oil use.

Depending on how much time you have, you should let the rub sit on the steak for at least 40 minutes, up to overnight. I personally use a sweet spot of about an hour: meaning that 1 hour prior to cooking, I take my steak out, rub it, then put it on a rack in the refrigerator to dry and absorb the flavor and spice from the rub. I prefer to make my own rubs vs. the store-bought versions that often contain hidden, nasty ingredients like MSG, gluten, and sugar.

There are thousands of different rub blend options, but I'm going to give you three of my favorite steak rubs, which, if you make extra, also go quite well with scrambled eggs the next morning, and can also successfully be used on other meats, such as chicken or fish.

For all resources, books, tools, and ingredients mentioned throughout this chapter go to:
BoundlessCookbook.com/steakrubs

BLACK SALT RUB

There's just something about the coarse black salt that I bring back after my hunting trips to Kona that lends a unique flavor to a good rub.

Use equal parts of the spices below, with enough volume to generously coat your meat on all sides. I tend to "eyeball" my ingredients, so exact measurements aren't necessary. For example, if you want a bit more of a spicy kick, throw in more cayenne. If you want to give it an Eastern twist, mix in a bit of cumin, curry, turmeric, or coriander. You get the idea: be creative and don't be afraid to break the rules a bit. Just be sure to use high-quality, organic spices without added fillers and preservatives.

Ingredients - Equal Parts Of:

Kona black salt   Cayenne

Black pepper   Paprika

RUB-WITH-A-KICK

If you ask my wife, she'll tell you I tend to go a bit overboard on the hot spices, but what can I say? I'm a fan of capsaicin, and it has a host of health benefits too, including a boost in your cell-protecting heat shock proteins and metabolic rate.

If I use a spicy rub mix like this, I like to toss in a few jalapeno peppers on the side of my meat to kick it up another notch. Like the other rubs, you can eyeball the ingredients, but I tend to use equal parts of the following:

Ingredients - Equal Parts Of:

Cayenne powder   Black pepper

Paprika   Garlic salt

Turmeric   Ginger powder

COFFEE RUB

Coffee is not only my most favorite legal drug of all time, but it's also a potent antioxidant that may limit some of the carcinogenic potential of a cooked piece of meat (you know, those blackened and charred bits that inevitably appear when you're grilling or high-heat cooking). One day, I figured I'd try out a bit of finely ground organic coffee in a rub and the result was nothing short of amazing. I haven't personally noticed any effects from the trace amounts of caffeine keeping me up at night after having a steak dinner, but you could theoretically use decaf coffee if you want to play it safe.

Ingredients

4 parts finely-ground organic coffee (I use just enough to cover the meat with a thin layer)

1 part salt (the black salt above works well, but I also dig Celtic salt and Colima salt for coarse, crunchy options that fit perfectly into a rub)

1 part Ceylon cinnamon

Cayenne, to taste

Instructions

In a small bowl, combine the ingredients above.

03

FISH

When it comes to fish, I'm a total "SMASH Diet" guy. As you can read more details about in my book *Boundless*, particularly in Chapter 4, choosing fish and other fat sources with a high omega-3 fatty acid composition can pay dividends for your cellular health, mitochondria, and anti-inflammatory powers.

The term "SMASH" refers to the fish that tend to be low in metals such as mercury, but particularly high in omega-3's: salmon, mackerel, anchovies, sardines, and herring. SMASH fish are all small fish, and that's important because the larger the fish and the longer its lifespan, the higher its mercury content due to the accumulation of metal from eating other smaller fish.

So whenever you have the option, **choose the smaller SMASH fish over larger predatory fish,** such as sea bass, tuna, mahi-mahi, etc. (Seafoodwatch.org is a wonderful source for discovering which fish are sustainably sourced and low in metals.)

SMASH fish are also rich in Docosahexaenoic Acid (DHA), a particularly helpful omega-3 fatty acid required for proper brain functioning. Beyond omega-3 fats, another benefit of eating SMASH fish is their favorable impact on the gut microbiome, and the extra bone-building minerals you consume if you're munching on the tiny, soft edible bones of these fish.

My favorite, convenient source for my SMASH recipes is Wild Planet, which produces low-metal, sustainably sourced fish preserved in wonderful spices, marinaras, and olive oils. These cans and boxes of Wild Planet fish currently crowd out about half the shelves in my pantry! If you're consuming a wide variety of SMASH fish, you should also stock your pantry with sea vegetables such as nori, hijiki, wakame, arame, and kombu that offer a good boost to your thyroid function, are chock-full of minerals, and perhaps, most importantly, have a wonderful umami flavor that pairs particularly well with fish. For sashimi grade fish, I recommend Seatopia.

For all resources, books, tools, and ingredients mentioned throughout this chapter go to:
BoundlessCookbook.com/fish

SALMON CAKES

If you've ever eaten at a restaurant that brings out crab cakes or salmon cakes as an appetizer, then you know two things: A) they're addictively good; B) they tend to be disappointingly small. But that's not the way I make my salmon cakes.

I use the Wild Planet cans of sockeye or pink salmon or Vital Choice Wild Alaskan Pink Salmon. Simply mix with a few key ingredients that you'll discover below, then form into enormous patties that are stunningly flavorful, quite appetite-satiating, and perfectly paired over a fried sushi rice cake and a bed of sprouts or vegetables. These are really fantastic served over a mushed-up sushi rice cake that you can grill in oil at the same time you're cooking your salmon cakes, or for a low-carb option the same approach, but with Miracle Noodle rice.

Total Time

20 minutes

Ingredients

2 (6-ounce) cans of wild salmon, drained*

½ cup gluten-free flour such as coconut, almond, or breadfruit flour

1 large egg

1½ tablespoons healthy mayonnaise

¾ teaspoon Dijon mustard

½ teaspoon Worcestershire sauce

½ teaspoon paprika and/or, for added spice, cayenne

2 tablespoons chopped green onion or celery

1 pinch sea salt

Unsweetened coconut flakes (optional, for dredging)

1 tablespoon avocado oil, for cooking

*Notes

I prefer to use Vital Choice Wild Alaskan Pink Salmon. One can is enough for 3-4 patties, depending on how big you make them.

Instructions

1. Place the drained canned salmon in a large mixing bowl and break up with a fork. Add the coconut, almond, or breadfruit flour, which helps to thicken the mixture and will keep your patties from falling apart as you cook them.
2. Whisk the egg in a small mixing bowl. Add the mayo, Dijon mustard, Worcestershire sauce, spice, green onion, and salt to the egg. Mix well to combine.

3. For added texture (this is a recommended step to include), dredge the salmon cakes in coconut flakes so that they have an outer coating of coconut flakes prior to adding to the skillet. You'll just need to keep a close eye on your salmon cakes to ensure the coconut flakes on the exterior surface don't burn.

4. Heat 1 tablespoon of the oil over medium-high heat in a cast-iron or stainless steel skillet.

5. Place the salmon cakes into the hot skillet and cook for 3-4 minutes per side, or until golden brown. Serve over a bed of greens or a rice cake with tartar sauce (Primal Kitchen has a great option for that, too.) or your favorite barbecue sauce, ketchup, or mayo. You can also break these up for lunch leftovers the next day and wrap burrito-style in a nori wrap!

LAZY MAN'S SUSHI
HAND ROLL

Look, I'm a huge fan of sushi, but it can be painstakingly time consuming to prepare. Enter my Lazy Man's Sushi Hand Roll: a giant appetite satiating roll that gives you all the flavor of a sushi roll with very little prep time.

This is a favorite lunchtime staple of mine when I'm not eating my big-ass lunchtime salad. It incorporates the wonderful Miracle Noodle rice, which uses natural soluble fiber found in the konjac flour called glucomannan. This special rice not only slows your digestion and prolongs the sensation of fullness, but it also contains virtually no calories and no carbohydrates.

I also use my friend Dr. Thomas Cowan's Garden Sea Vegetable Powder in this recipe, which is a blend of dulse, wakame, and kelp, all harvested off the coast of Maine, certified organic, and thoroughly tested for any trace of contamination by such things as heavy metals and radiation. It's packed with vital nutrients, omega-3 fats, fat-soluble carotenoids, a compound called fucoxanthin, which inhibits the accumulation of fat in cells, and sodium alginate (which has been shown to reduce the absorption of radiation from the gut by 50-80%, an important ally when you're consuming fish, since much of the ocean contains irradiated materials).

Total Time

15 minutes

Tools And Materials

Cast iron skillet

Ingredients

1 packet Miracle Noodle rice*

Extra virgin olive oil, about a teaspoon

1 dollop (about 2 tablespoons), Primal Kitchen Mayonnaise (their pesto or aioli versions are good for this)

1 can Wild Planet sardines or tuna

Dr. Cowan's Garden Sea Vegetable Powder, to taste

A good salt such as Celtic or Colima salt, to taste

Black pepper, to taste

Nori wraps (use a metal-free brand, such as Emerald Cove)

*Notes

There is a "firm" option that I prefer for this recipe and other sushi-esque recipes versus their softer versions. One packet will be enough for 2 wraps.

Instructions

1. Rinse and strain the rice, then heat in a cast iron skillet over a little bit of olive oil.
2. Add a large dollop mayonnaise and an entire can of Wild Planet fish.
3. Heat at about low to medium, stirring every 30 seconds or so. While heating, season to taste with sea vegetable powder, salt, and black pepper.
4. Remove from the heat, spoon or spatula into a bowl or onto a plate, then wrap burrito-style with the nori wrap. If you want, you can use a sushi bamboo mat to help you roll up your ingredients, but I find it simple enough to just wrap with my hands.
5. Optionally, you can add a little bit of wasabi to kick up the spice factor or sprinkle in a few chopped macadamia nuts for some added crunch and calories. I usually mow down 2 of these wraps for lunch.

SOUS VIDE
SALMON

The mouth-watering tenderness of a sous vide cook on a high-quality, wild-caught salmon is to die for. I dig this recipe with a side of sweet potato or carrot fries (recipe on page 86), served over a bed of fresh sprouts and other vegetables or a large salad.

Total Time

1 hour

Tools And Materials

Sous vide wand

Silicone Stasher bags

Ingredients

Wild-caught salmon, cut into whatever fillet size you desire*

2 tablespoons extra virgin olive oil, divided

Dill, about 1 teaspoon

1 lemon, juiced

A good salt, to taste

Pepper, to taste

*Notes

I usually get my salmon from US Wellness Meats or Seatopia.

Instructions

1. You already know how to sous vide based on the steak recipe earlier in this cookbook (page 16). The only modifications you'll make for this recipe are as follows:
    *   No "pre-sear" of the salmon required.
    *   Use 122 °F.
    *   Sous vide for 40-50 minutes.
2. Once your salmon is cooked, you have the option to give the filets a quick sear (using 1 tablespoon of olive oil) on a cast iron skillet to crisp up the skin, which I highly recommend.

SPAM
MUSUBI

Spam musubi is a popular snack and lunch food in Hawaii composed of a slice of grilled spam served on top of a block of rice and wrapped with nori in the tradition of what the Japanese call "omusubi." It's inexpensive, it's portable, and it's found near many, many cash registers in convenience stores spread all over Hawaii. Although not a "fish dish" per se, it's so prevalently consumed in seafood-eating areas that it seemed fitting here.

But let's face it: store-bought spam and gas station-bought spam musubi ain't exactly healthy. Spam's basic ingredients are cheap, poorly-sourced pork mixed with ham, salt, water, sugar, and modified potato starch to bind it. It's preserved with sodium nitrite and packaged for months up to years in a metal-lined can.

On a bowhunting trip to Hawaii, my twin boys absolutely fell in love with these tasty snacks and then decided to figure out how to make their own amazingly healthy version of a spam musubi. I later discovered that the same spam "blocks" used to make this recipe actually freeze quite easily and can also be a wonderful chopped or sliced addition to scrambled eggs!

You'll need sushi rice and eggs to make this musubi complete.

SUSHI RICE

Sushi rice is quite simple to make. You'll need:

Ingredients

2 cups uncooked glutinous white rice (sushi rice)

3 cups water

½ cup rice vinegar

1 tablespoon vegetable oil

1 teaspoon salt

¼ cup white sugar (sugar is optional but really helps with the texture.)

Total Time

30 minutes

Instructions

1. Simply rinse your sushi rice in a strainer or colander until the water runs clear, then combine with water in a medium saucepan.
2. Bring to a boil, then reduce the heat to low, cover, and cook for 20 minutes. The rice should now be tender and the water should be absorbed. Cool the rice enough to handle (about 5 minutes).
3. Next, in a small saucepan, combine the rice vinegar, oil, sugar, and salt. Cook over medium heat until the sugar dissolves.
4. Cool, then stir into the cooked rice. When you pour this into the rice it will seem very wet. Keep stirring until the rice is dry and cool.

You'll also need 4 scrambled eggs and nori. You can find the recipe for perfect scrambled eggs on page 60.

OK, on to the spam musubis!

Total Time

2 hours 30 minutes

Tools And Materials

Loaf pan

Cake pan

Aluminum foil to cover

Musubi maker

Ingredients

4 ounces ham (from a healthy pork source)

¾ cup water, divided

1½ pounds ground organic pastured pork

2 teaspoons salt

2 teaspoons coconut sugar

3 tablespoons tapioca starch

4 cups of water for the water bath

Nori

Instructions

1. Process the ham and ¼ cup of water in a food processor or blender until it forms a paste.
2. Add the raw ground pork and ½ cup of water, salt, sugar, and starch, until a thick paste is formed.
3. Transfer into a bowl, and refrigerate for at least 1 hour.
4. Preheat the oven to 400 °F.
5. Press the spam into a 9 x 5 x 3-inch loaf pan with the back of a spoon. Place the loaf pan into a cake pan.
6. Boil 4 cups of water on the stovetop. Pour the boiling water into the cake pan. The water level should go about halfway up the sides of the loaf pan (this is called a water bath).
7. Cover the loaf pan with aluminum foil. This will ensure that your spam remains moist. I have yet to be concerned about toxic aluminum levels from the use of aluminum foil while cooking. But, if you're concerned, instead of the foil, use parchment paper, a baking sheet, a silicone lid or mat, or a metal lid.
8. Bake for 50-60 minutes, then remove the spam from the loaf pan and cool for about 10 minutes.

Musubi Construction

Now that your spam is ready, it's time to prepare your nori, and combine it with the sushi rice and scrambled eggs.

1. Cut the nori lengthwise.
2. To construct the roll, you will lay out a half sheet of nori.
3. Place the musubi maker on a short end of the nori.
4. Spoon your sushi rice into the musubi maker, and then use the provided press to press the rice down.
5. Next, slice a bit of spam and lay it on top of the rice.
6. The next layer will be a heaping spoonful of the scrambled eggs.
7. To finish the layers you will add a small layer of rice. Finally, take the press and press all the layers down.

Now lift up the musubi maker mold and wrap the nori around your spam-rice-egg stack. Seal the nori like an envelope and... voila! Your spam musubi is ready to devour. For extra flavor and kick, I personally like these drizzled with a bit of a good hot sauce, or with cayenne pepper sprinkled inside.

04

WILD GAME

Ever since I began bowhunting for animals such as whitetail deer, elk, wild boar, goat, and even scrub cattle in Hawaii, I have always loved the rugged, natural taste of well-prepared wild game.

When I interviewed nutritionist Teri Cochrane about wild game, she highlighted several benefits that she details in her excellent book *Wildatarian*, including:

- The rise of the modern meat production industry, with its crowded spaces, supplemental hormones, antibiotics, and herbicides and pesticides, has significantly modified not only the quality of conventional meat products but their composition on a molecular level.

- Research suggests that the protein structures within conventionally produced meat and poultry possess the tendency to become truncated and misfolded into protein structures known as amyloids. Over time, our bodies have shown difficulty in the assimilation of these altered protein structures. The heightened presence of amyloids in the body is linked to innumerable chronic diseases — including Type I diabetes, Alzheimer's, Parkinson's, and autoimmune disease. These amyloids are not destroyed even with a high-temperature cooking process.

- Despite what nature intended, **the food we eat has gone from nourishing to devastating.** Research shows that mice fed amyloid-affected beef succumb to amyloidosis within weeks. Amyloidosis is a disease state where the amyloid proteins build up in organs and tissues. The stressful conditions these animals live in create chronic inflammation in their tissues. The repeated rounds of hormones and antibiotics and grain-based diet shifts their otherwise neutral stomach pH toward acidity, lowers their immune function, and promotes illness and disease necessitating the constant dosing of antibiotics.

- Commercially raised beef contains primarily omega-6 fatty acids, and virtually no beneficial omega-3s. Omega-6 fatty acids, while essential, can contribute to inflammation when present in high amounts. High levels of omega-6 fatty acids have been linked to arthritis and other inflammatory disease states.

- Domesticated animals typically contain higher fat content. Fat stores xenoestrogens — industrially-made compounds that mimic the hormone estrogen. Therefore, these higher-fat animals may store higher levels of xenoestrogens. When we eat this meat, these hormone disruptors are then stored in our fatty tissue. Xenoestrogens are now suspected to be linked to many health issues, including uterine fibroids, PCOS, menstrual irregularities, and even hormonal cancers.

The significance of the amyloids in the food supply and their contribution to disease states, makes Teri's argument for the consumption of wild-caught meats, fish, and shellfish quite compelling.

Think about it this way: thousands of years ago, animal meats were hunted in their natural habitats. They lived and grazed in ample non-crowded spaces. So wild game is the original grass-fed, free-range, sustainable meat source! Most wild game is leaner, relatively higher in omega-3 fatty acids, and often lower in cholesterol, making it a better protein source for people who suffer from inflammatory diseases. These meats are not tainted by steroids, antibiotics, and other additives. Additionally, wild game is richer in minerals, especially zinc, selenium, and iron due, in part, to their natural wild vegetation diet as opposed to the grain and corn fed to domesticated animals. Because they are not raised in crowded, toxic conditions, their meat is more bioavailable to us.

Are you convinced yet that wild meat should be a major part of your protein sources? You can find wild meat, fish, and foul selections at most larger grocers. National chains such as Costco, Food Lion, Giant, Harris Teeter, Kroger, and Publix, as well as Trader Joe's and Whole Foods also carry a surprising selection of wild game.

At mainstream stores, the typical wild animal proteins you will find include: buffalo, lamb, bison, Cornish game hen, duck, wild fish, and shellfish. Smaller specialty stores might also include wild boar, pheasant, venison, antelope, elk, and other wild cuts. Your local farmer's market is another perfect place to look. Having a friend or family member who hunts is another option. Finally, in addition to meat resources you'll find on page 13, online providers such as the following are other options for wild game:

- Wild Idea Buffalo Company
- Fossil Farms
- The Spruce Eats sources providers of wild game

Following, you'll find three of my favorite wild game recipes.

For all resources, books, tools, and ingredients mentioned throughout this chapter go to:
BoundlessCookbook.com/wildgame

AXIS RIB
ROAST

My annual Axis deer bowhunting trips to Hawaii are a true highlight of my hunting year, and although these critters are very fast, super smart, and difficult to harvest, their meat is widely considered among hunters to be some of the best-tasting, most tender wild game meat on the face of the planet. This rib roast is one of my favorite ways to prepare one of the best bits of the axis deer I work so hard for every year, and can also work on the rib of any wild game.

Total Time

Dry age: 24 hours (optional) | Roast: 55 minutes

Ingredients

1 venison roast, about 2 pounds

1-2 tablespoons extra virgin olive oil

Sea salt, to taste

Freshly ground black pepper, to taste

6-8 ribs celery (you'll use these to make a roast holder)

Chimichurri Sauce

¾ cup extra virgin olive oil

½ cup white wine vinegar

6 cloves garlic

3 bay leaves

2 jalapeño peppers, stemmed, seeded, and chopped

½ cup tightly packed fresh cilantro

½ cup tightly packed fresh flat-leaf parsley

¼ cup tightly packed fresh oregano leaves

1 tablespoon sea salt

1 tablespoon ancho chile powder

1 teaspoon freshly ground black pepper

Instructions

1. This step is optional but will give your meat superior texture. A day prior to cooking, pat the roast dry with paper towels, place it on a rack over a small pan to catch the drips, and put into the refrigerator, uncovered, to dry-age for at least 24 hours. Then, 1 hour prior to cooking, remove the roast from the refrigerator and let it come to room temperature.

2. **Chimichurri sauce:** Combine all the ingredients in a food processor or blender, and process to desired texture. Transfer to a small bowl, cover with plastic wrap, and refrigerate until you begin roasting the meat. Serve at room temperature.

3. Preheat your oven (or grill — I like to use a Traeger grill for most of my wild game as the smoking effect enhances the flavor of the leaner cuts of meat) to 400 °F. Lightly coat the rib roast with oil, salt, and pepper.

4. In a cast iron skillet large enough that the roast doesn't touch the sides, over medium-high heat, lightly sear all surfaces, using tongs to turn the meat and to hold it in place while searing.

5. Remove the meat from the skillet and set aside. This next part is fun, and just like building with Lincoln Logs! Simply fashion a rack inside the skillet with the celery ribs. This should hold the roast up so that no part of the meat is touching the skillet.

6. Place the skillet in the oven and roast for 20-25 minutes, or until a meat thermometer placed in the thickest part of the roast reads 125 °F. Then remove, transfer to your serving dish or cutting board, and let rest for 10 minutes.

7. Carve however you desire (I simply cut it into individual ribs), and serve drizzled with the chimichurri sauce.

BRAISED
BOAR BELLY

The wild boar I hunt in Hawaii, unlike the subpar tasting pigs I've hunted in Texas, is rich and flavorful — probably due to the nutrient and fat-dense diet of foods such as native plants, mangos, avocados, and macadamia nuts the pigs feed on in the relatively low-stress environment of the island of Hawaii. This braised boar belly will melt in your mouth and keep you coming back for more.

Total Time

Brine: overnight or 8 hours
1 hour 40 minutes

Tools And Materials

A braising pan or pot

Ingredients

2 pounds wild boar belly*

~1 quart beef or chicken broth (enough to cover the meat)

4 cups brining solution (just add about 6 tablespoons of good salt to 4 cups of cold water)

A good cooking oil such as extra virgin olive oil or avocado oil

*Notes

If you can't find wild boar belly, you can use pastured pork belly as a replacement. I get mine from BelCampo Meats.

Instructions

1. Brine the boar belly in the solution overnight in your fridge.
2. Preheat your oven to 325 °F.
3. Cut the belly into pieces that aren't too big to lay into your braising pan in a single layer.
4. Score the belly fat in a shallow crisscross pattern on the non-rib side.
5. Get the oil hot in a pan over medium/medium-high heat.
6. Lay the pieces of belly in the pan fat-side down, and sear. This will render out the fat.
7. Flip the belly once it has developed a brown crust, and quickly sear the other side.
8. Pour off the excess fat into a separate container like a shallow glass jar (you can use this later as fat for recipes like scrambled eggs, steaks, etc.), and then pour in enough beef or chicken broth to cover the belly.
9. Cover the pan, and bring the broth to a simmer.
10. Move the pan to the oven to braise for 1½ hours, until tender.
11. I like to heavily salt this belly and then serve over cubed and baked squash, yam or sweet potato, or over any cooked and pureed root vegetable.

MUTTON
LEG ROAST

Mutton, by definition, tends to come from sheep that are older than 1 year and often older than 3 years old. The meat has a deep red color and is much fattier than lamb. But the meat can be tough, strongly flavored, and somewhat gamy, especially when it comes from the wild sheep I hunt in Hawaii.

For these reasons, mutton is often stewed to help tenderize it, but I've found a long roast with a generous layering of fat to also do the trick. If you marinate overnight prior to cooking, it's even better. This is quite simple: just toss into a blender or food processor a generous amount of onion, ginger, garlic cloves, Dijon mustard (optional, but lends good flavor), the squeeze of 1 or a few lemons, and enough apple cider vinegar to submerge the mutton, and let it sit for about 8 hours.

For a more Eastern flavor, you can also include in your marinade mustard powder, turmeric, dry red chili powder, coriander powder, and cumin powder. Oh, and one last tip to tenderize meat: if you're short on marinade ingredients, break open 4-6 digestive enzymes capsules (yep the same you would eat prior to a meal) and sprinkle them over the meat with some lemon juice and vinegar, then let sit for at least a couple hours, or preferably overnight. These enzymes do a surprisingly good job at tenderizing meat and "pre-digesting" some of the fibrous protein.

Total Time

Normal roast: 1 hour 10 minutes
Pot roast: 5-6 hours 10 minutes

Tools And Materials

A large roasting tray, ideally deep sides and handles

Meat thermometer

Aluminum foil

Ingredients

Leg of mutton*

*Notes

You can also use sheep or goat. Refer to the resource section at the back of this book for sources.

Marinade

Onion

Ginger

Garlic cloves

Dijon mustard (optional, but lends good flavor)

Lemons

Apple cider vinegar (enough to submerge the leg)

Mustard powder

Turmeric

Dry red chili powder

Coriander powder

Cumin powder

Generous amounts of each according to your taste

Roast

Any good fat (I highly recommend goose or duck fat if possible)

Equal Amounts Of

Onion

Carrot

Celery

A bay leaf

Sprig of thyme

1-2 cloves garlic, chopped

A handful black peppercorns

Instructions

1. Pat the thawed leg of mutton dry and bring to room temperature on a large, roasting tray, ideally with deep sides and handles for easy movement.
2. Preheat your oven (or grill) to 400 ºF.
3. Massage the leg with any good fat (if you can find it, I like goose or duck fat) or olive oil, then season with high-quality salt such as coarse Kona Black Salt, Colima Mexican Salt, or Celtic Salt.
4. Make an elevated surface for the leg to rest upon by chopping equal amounts of onion, carrot, and celery, along with a bay leaf, sprig of thyme, chopped clove or two of garlic, and a handful of black peppercorns, then position the leg on top of these chopped ingredients.
5. Place in the center of the oven, and roast for 20 minutes. Reduce the temperature to 375 ºF and continue roasting for 30 minutes until a meat thermometer measures the thickest part of the leg at 150 ºF.
6. Alternatively, you can also add half a bottle of red or white wine and an equal amount of water to the tray and, after the first 20 minutes, cover with foil and pot roast at 275 ºF for 5-6 hours, nice and slow.
7. Remove from the oven, cover, and allow to rest for a minimum of 20 minutes before carving, leaving the roasted vegetables in the tray for the gravy.

For the gravy, stir all the caramelized juices out from the tray and into a clean saucepan. You can use a sieve to push all the juices from the vegetables into the saucepan, too. Then bring the saucepan to a simmer and thicken by whisking in a teaspoon or two of non-GMO corn flour mixed with a few splashes of cold water. Allow to simmer away until you get a nice, thick glossy gravy and then drizzle this rich goodness over the roast.

05

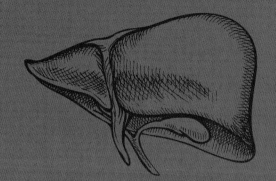

ORGAN MEAT

Yes, yes, I know: eating organ meat (also called "offal") sounds gross or, well, awful. But as you're about to learn, **organ meats can be prepared in amazingly flavorful ways**. And, when you think about it, there's a solid ethical and environmental argument for eating an entire animal "nose-to-tail" rather than wasting the majority of an animal (the organs, bones, skin, and other miscellaneous parts) to simply eat the muscle meat.

In my opinion, however, **the health benefits of organ meats are the most compelling reason to consume these odd bits**. There are two important considerations here:

1. Protein balance

All proteins are comprised of protein-building blocks called amino acids. Methionine is the amino acid found mostly in muscle meat and eggs, while glycine is the amino acid found mostly in organ meat and bones. It's particularly high in the gelatinous rich components of an animal such as the ears, tail, and skin that are usually used in bone broth.

Most modern protein consumers, due to a diet shifted in an unbalanced manner toward primarily muscle meat consumption, are eating tons of methionine and barely any glycine. Why is this a problem? It turns out that studies show methionine restriction can increase lifespan and improve most factors of metabolic health, such as body fat, insulin sensitivity, blood lipids, and liver health. But getting more glycine into the diet can help balance out these excess methionine levels.

2. Nutrient density

Organ meats are truly "nature's multivitamin," with a much higher nutrient density than common so-called "superfoods" such as kale, blueberries, spirulina, or any other fancy overpriced fad plant. Organ meats are particularly good sources of B-vitamins, such as vitamin B12 and folate. They are packed full of minerals, including magnesium, iron, zinc, and selenium. And, they also contain important fat-soluble vitamins like vitamins A, D, E, and K.

Finally, should you be concerned about the myth that organ meats such as kidneys and liver are "filters" and you'll be consuming toxins... don't be. These organs don't filter toxins by trapping them in tissue and keeping them there, but rather by shunting them out into urine and feces, where they quickly exit the body. So unless you're eating an animal's bladder and colon, you'll be just fine (although, as with all meat, I still recommend you get organ meats from clean, grass-fed, grass-finished sources).

Convinced that you may want to work a few organ meats into your diet? I personally consume some type of offal three to five times a week. Following are two of my favorite ways of preparing these foods:

For all resources, books, tools, and ingredients mentioned throughout this chapter go to:
BoundlessCookbook.com/organmeat

LIVER AND
ONIONS

While the cooking tactic you're about to learn works particularly well for liver, I've successfully thin sliced and dredged everything from heart to kidney to testicle using the same method. Just don't skip the soaking step: it will remove any gamy flavor from the organ meats and make them far more tender and palatable.

Total Time

Soak: 24 hours | Cooking: 30 minutes

Ingredients For The Marinade

1½ pounds beef, chicken, or lamb liver

Kefir or raw milk

Lemon juice

Apple cider vinegar

Ingredients For The Liver

½ cup any gluten-free flour (I use coconut or breadfruit flour)

1 teaspoon black pepper

½ teaspoon good salt

3 tablespoons extra virgin olive oil

2 onions, sliced thin

1 cup beef or chicken broth

1-2 tablespoons cornstarch

Instructions

1. Soak the liver for 24 hours in kefir (page 125), raw milk, or a half/half blend of lemon juice and apple cider vinegar. This results in a wonderful, soft texture and eliminates any gamy liver flavor.
2. Rinse the marinade off the liver with water, then slice it into ½-inch thick slices.
3. Put the flour, pepper, and salt into a bowl large enough to dredge the pieces of liver through, and then use a fork to mix the ingredients thoroughly.
4. Dredge the liver slices in the flour. Dredging is simply a cooking technique used to coat wet or moist foods with a dry ingredient prior to cooking. You simply place the liver slice into the flour and turn it over to make sure that it's coated on all sides. Sometimes, prior to dredging the liver, I'll dip it into a whipped up egg to allow the flour, salt, and pepper to stick to it better, but this step isn't necessary. It does seem to lend a bit of additional flavor and texture, however.
5. Remove any excess flour by gently shaking each slice of liver as you take it out. A light flour coating is all you need.
6. Heat the extra virgin olive oil in a large skillet on medium-high heat for 1-2 minutes.
7. Place the liver slices into the skillet in a single layer. Make sure that they don't overlap. Cook each side of the liver for 1-2 minutes. Use kitchen tongs to turn the slice over after the side has browned.

8. If space permits, you can cook your sliced onions on the skillet at the same time as the liver, or in a separate skillet on the side. I'll often use butter instead of olive oil for the onions, and I like to brown the onions for a total of about 5 minutes on medium-high heat.

9. Pour the broth into the skillet with the liver. Add the onions (if you've cooked them in a separate skillet), and use a wooden spoon to mix them all together.

10. Reduce the heat to low, and cover the skillet with a lid. Simmer the ingredients until the onions are tender and the broth has thickened, which should take about 10-15 minutes.

11. Before removing the skillet from the heat, check that the liver is cooked. Make a small cut into the thickest part of a liver slice. It should be slightly pink in the middle with brown edges (slightly pink means that it's not overcooked). If it looks rare or raw, continue cooking it for a few minutes more and check it again. You can also use a meat thermometer to check if the liver is cooked. Insert it into the thickest part of the liver and check that the temperature has reached at least 165 °F.

12. Serve the liver with the sauteed onions on top of the slices and gravy poured over that or on the side.

There are a few twists on this recipe. Sometimes I add bacon, which seems to go quite well with the liver, by cooking it also on the side then crumbling crispy bacon over the top of the liver, onions, and gravy. I'll also sometimes add a bit of cornstarch to thicken the gravy. Finally, this pairs well with sauteed or steamed greens, such as beet greens, spinach, kale, or bok choy.

"NATURE'S MULTIVITAMIN"
BREAKFAST BURRITO

This breakfast burrito method is a great way to eat organ meats and get all the nutrient density of these superfoods for breakfast (or, if you're like me, occasionally for dinner), without some of the off-putting taste that some people associate or experience when eating organ meats.

Think about this the same way you might think about "hiding" vegetables by blending them into a kid's spaghetti sauce. Speaking of kids, my boys also love to have this meal for breakfast, and I love that they can consume a hefty portion of organ meats, yet not have their little palates rebel against the taste of the organ meats. When it comes to the eggs part of this recipe, be sure to choose your eggs carefully and ideally get pasture-raised and certified organic only. (For more, see my write up on chickens on page 62.)

Total Time

12 minutes

Ingredients

US Wellness Meats' Beef Braunschweiger or Liverwurst or Head Cheese* - as many slices or cubed chunks as you desire.

Eggs (as many as you'd like to scramble)

A tablespoon or two of these heat stable, healthy oils: extra virgin olive oil, coconut oil, ghee, butter, lard or macadamia nut oil

Sliced avocado (optional, but lends great flavor)

Organic ketchup (I use Primal Kitchen Ketchup) or salsa (Thrive Market has a ton of good organic salsa options)

Almond flour wrap

Spices (I like cayenne, paprika, black pepper, and a good coarse salt)

*Notes

The Braunschweiger is a 60/40 mix of grass-fed trim and grass-fed beef liver. It comes in a fully cooked, 1-pound package and is ready to slice and serve. Beef Braunschweiger is milder than Liverwurst, so it is great if you are new to incorporating organ meats into your diet.

The Liverwurst is a mixture of grass-fed beef trim (50%), liver (20%), heart (20%), and kidney (10%).

The Head Cheese (not the greatest name, in my opinion) is a mix of grass-fed beef heart (15%), tongue (15%), and trim (70%) with a robust, smooth flavor. It also comes in a fully cooked, 1-pound roll ready for you to slice and enjoy, or add to these scrambled eggs. All three are free of soy, sweetener, dairy, MSG, additives, binders, and preservatives.

Instructions

Make scrambled eggs as you would normally make any scrambled eggs. (I personally think the very best scrambled eggs recipes and variations are to be found at MrBreakfast.com and also in Tim Ferriss's *4-Hour Chef* book.) In case you haven't made scrambled eggs before, here's how I nail them perfectly:

PERFECTLY SCRAMBLED EGGS

1. Use the freshest eggs you can find, always organic and free-range.
2. In a mixing bowl, whip the eggs thoroughly so that you combine the whites and yolks for a streak-free scramble. This will also get a good amount of air into the mix for ultra-light, tender eggs, which is key. Then season the eggs with a little bit of salt.
3. Use medium-low to low heat and a cast iron or better yet, stainless steel skillet. High heat makes for more dry, tough proteins and can even oxidize or damage some of the fats in the eggs, while lower heat will give you a soft custardy scramble.
4. Use butter as your cooking fat for the eggs. Nothing beats the moisture of butter to amplify the flavor and texture of your scramble.
5. Once the butter is melted, add your very well-beaten eggs and let them sit for just a second. This whole process takes about a minute and a half, so every second counts.
6. Use a spatula or wooden spoon to push the eggs from one side of the skillet to the other, sweeping the spatula all the way around the edge of the skillet to create long waves.
7. Continue to do this, tilting the skillet if necessary to spread any uncooked egg over the surface of the skillet, until the eggs are mostly done but seem slightly undercooked (like any proteins, they'll keep cooking between skillet and plate). This shouldn't take longer than 2 minutes. Then, get them off that hot skillet and onto your breakfast plate!

I usually throw my avocados and spices into the pan (with butter) first, cook them for about 5 minutes then put them into a separate bowl, add more butter, cook the eggs using the method described above, then just as my eggs finish, toss the spiced avocadoes back in, and add a few extra spices to the blend for added flavor once I scrape it all off the pan.

In a separate pan, over your healthy cooking oil of choice, slice or cube the organ meats and brown for about 2 or 3 minutes each side from medium to high heat. Then toss them onto your plate over the scrambled eggs and avocado, top with ketchup and/or salsa, and wrap everything into the almond flour tortilla.

For an extra step, you can lightly toast your tortilla in your egg pan or organ meat pan for 1-2 minutes per side. Optionally, for a lower calorie "burrito-esque" option you can forego the almond tortilla and instead wrap in a seaweed nori wrap.

06

CHICKEN

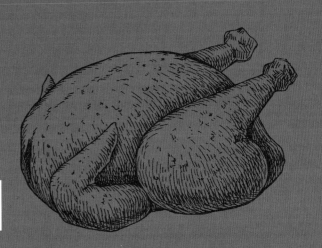

Although I don't consider chicken to be the most nutrient-dense of meats, I have a special place in my heart for my wife's fabulous roasted chicken, and also dig the simplicity, ease, and digestibility of a well-prepared chicken meal. So I tend to eat chicken two to three times a week.

But not all chicken is created equal! The sad fact is that **commercially-raised poultry live in shockingly inhumane conditions,** stuck in tight-fitting cages for most of their lives, and given a variety of medications to increase feed utilization and accelerate growth. These stressed birds undergo spontaneous amyloidosis due to a chronic inflammatory response that causes amyloid fibrils to form non-functioning deposits of this protein-like material in their organs. See the section on wild meat in this cookbook (page 43) to understand more about why that's such a concerning issue.

So is the answer to ensure you hunt down free-range, organic chickens, or eggs from those types of chickens? Not necessarily!

See, all free-range means, especially when buying at the average supermarket, is that the chickens are factory farmed in operations with tens of thousands of hens who very occasionally get to roam "free" on a tiny concrete patio for a few minutes or hours daily!

When these hens are raised in these indoor, crowded conditions, they aren't out eating their natural diet of insects, green plants, wild seeds, and worms and so the farmer is forced to bring the food to the hens. That food is... drumroll please... grains! These grains, particularly corn and soy, even if organic, are especially problematic for the nutritional profile of both the chickens and the eggs they produce.

A grain or so-called "vegetarian" fed chicken contains much higher pro-inflammatory omega-6 fatty acid content, which produces inflammation in both the chicken, the eggs, and ultimately you.

Meanwhile, eggs that have been tested from true pasture-raised chickens have **200% more Omega-3 fatty acids, 300% more vitamin D, and 700% more beta carotene** than factory-farmed eggs. These pasture-raised chickens roam happily outside 365 days a year and are rotated onto fresh, well-managed land daily, rather than living their life walking around in their own fecal matter and eating environmentally and biologically damaging mono-crops like corn and soy.

So where can you find truly pasture-raised, organic chickens and eggs? If you're dead set on sticking to the supermarket, check out cornucopia.org. Click on the "scorecards" tab and then find the "eggs" tab. There you'll find a rating system for pretty much every egg brand you'll see at the supermarket. You can also check out eatwild.com. Click on the "shop local grass-fed meat, dairy, and eggs," then simply select your state.

For more on factory farming, ethical animal raising, regenerative farming practices, and other such tips, I recommend Evgeny Trufkin's book *Anti-Factory Farm Shopping Guide* and also the entire suite of books written by a farmer and former podcast guest of mine, Joel Salatin. Each of his books is incredibly humorous, eye-opening, and enlightening, and you'll learn a ton more about where your food comes from and how to choose it properly.

For all resources, books, tools, and ingredients mentioned throughout this chapter go to: BoundlessCookbook.com/chicken

BEER CAN CHICKEN

Tender, falling-off-the-bone, moist on the inside, crispy on the outside. That's what you can expect with beer can chicken, also known as beer butt chicken, or as my twin boys occasionally allude to and snicker at, sticking a brewski up a chicken's arse.

While the chicken is roasting and getting super crispy on the outside, the inside is being bathed with the steam from beer (or really, any other convenient liquid you choose), keeping the chicken meat tender and moist on the inside. If you don't have any beer lying around, just fill a pint Mason jar halfway with chicken broth or bone broth and use it instead of beer.

Total Time

1 hour 45 minutes

Ingredients For The Rub Mix

2 tablespoons garlic powder

2 teaspoons onion powder

2 teaspoons coconut sugar

1 teaspoon paprika

1 teaspoon chili powder

½ teaspoon ground chipotle

¼ teaspoon ground cinnamon

¼ teaspoon ground mustard seed

¼ teaspoon table salt

¼ teaspoon ground pepper

Ingredients For The Chicken

1 whole organic chicken, innards removed

1 bundle of fresh rosemary and thyme

3 tablespoons extra virgin olive oil (or avocado oil)

1 can of beer of your choice

Instructions

1. Preheat the oven or grill to 375 °F.
2. Mix all the ingredients for the rub in a bowl, and then massage the rub into every nook, cranny, and crevice of the chicken, along with a generous coating on the outside of the entire chicken. For optional extra flavor, you can tie a bundle of thyme and rosemary together and stuff it inside the cavity of the chicken (just remember to take the innards out of your chicken first).
3. Next, drizzle the chicken with olive oil and place the bundle of herbs into the chicken cavity.

4. Grab a chicken leg in each hand, then plunk the entire bird cavity over the beer can. Transfer the bird-on-a-can to your oven or grill, balancing the chicken on its 2 legs and the can like a tripod.
5. Cover and let cook for 1-1½ hours, checking the temperature every 25 minutes. The chicken is done when the internal temperature is 165 °F.

Remove from the grill or oven, and enjoy! This goes quite well with the carrot fries (page 86) or sweet potato fries (page 84) in this cookbook.

.70

JESSA'S WORLD-FAMOUS ROASTED CHICKEN

This is one of my wife's super-easy-to-prepare, go-to recipes after a long day of work, gardening, driving the boys around, and doing other activities that require a simple approach to dinner (albeit a quite tasty one). I just can't get enough of this roasted chicken, and go so far as to eat every last bit of crispy skin and even chew the joints off the end of the bones to suck every last bit of marrow out. It's *that* good.

Total Time

1 hour 15 minutes

Tools And Materials

Pastry brush

Ingredients For The Rub Mix

1 tablespoon celery flakes

1 tablespoon kosher salt

1 tablespoon paprika

1 tablespoon garlic powder

1 tablespoon onion powder

1 tablespoon ground thyme

2 teaspoons dried sage

1½ teaspoons ground black pepper

1½ teaspoons dried rosemary

½ teaspoon cayenne pepper

Ingredients For The Chicken

Rosemary

Thyme

Sage

Sliced lemon wedges

1 clove garlic

1 head onion

Extra virgin olive oil

Bacon fat, for basting, optional

Instructions

1. **To make the rub:** Stir all the ingredients for the rub together in a bowl. Then transfer the entire mixture to a spice grinder or food processor, and blend until smooth.

2. **For the chicken:** Preheat the oven to 450 °F. Stuff the carcass of the chicken with fresh herbs: rosemary, thyme, sage, sliced lemon wedges, a head of garlic, and onion.

3. Gently pull the skin away, or gently cut into the outer fascia layer with a knife, and cover as much of the layer as possible between the chicken muscle and skin with the spice rub.

4. Finally, use a pastry brush to spread a thin layer of olive oil over the entire exterior of the chicken.

5. Roast the chicken at 450 °F for the first 15 minutes, and then bring the heat down to 350 °F and roast for another 30 minutes.

6. During those 30 minutes, Jessa likes to baste the chicken with bacon fat (basting is simply pouring juices or melted fat over meat during cooking in order to keep it moist). This step is optional, but the big bonus is super crispy skin, even more than you get with the initial olive oil coating.

7. To finish the chicken, cook at 450 °F for a final 15 minutes, or until internal temp on the thickest part of the breast reads 165 °F.

07

BREAD

Bread is a comfort food, a staple, an appetizer, and a perfect way to soak up all the extra oils, spices, and sauces leftover on your plate after any of the delicious meals in this cookbook. But unless you've been hiding under a rock, you are no doubt familiar with the vilification of bread based on that pesky protein gluten.

Gluten is a general term for the proteins found in wheat. This includes wheat berries, emmer, durum, spelt, semolina, farina, graham flour, and farro. It's also found in rye, barley, and triticale (a cross between wheat and rye). Gluten acts as a glue to help foods keep their shape. But because of its inherent stickiness and ability to create digestive difficulties, gluten has become the ultimate pariah among health enthusiasts and hippies. While they are less common than many people claim, gluten intolerances, cross-reactivities, and allergies can be legitimate problems and can even cause serious health complications, such as gut damage, autoimmune diseases, and neuroinflammation.

Even if you don't have an intolerance or allergy to gluten, or if it doesn't seem to cause perceivable gut issues, **gluten can still damage your brain.** Dr. David Perlmutter, a renowned neurologist, wrote the book *Grain Brain* to reveal how excess carbohydrates, especially gluten-containing grains, can cause a host of neurological problems. These problems range from dysregulation of the autonomic nervous system (the part of your nervous system responsible for automatic actions such as breathing and digestion), cerebellar ataxia (inflammation of or damage to the cerebellum, which causes loss of fine motor skills), hypotonia (low muscle tone), developmental delay, learning disorders, depression, migraines, and headaches. In fact, research has connected gluten sensitivities to neurological and psychiatric concerns like autism, schizophrenia, and hallucinations.

Fortunately, you can minimize the effect of gluten on your brain and the rest of your nervous system. For example, gluten can be broken down before eating via fermentation, which is why some of the only bread I eat is my wife Jessa's mouthwatering homemade sourdough. Through the process of slow fermentation, sourdough lactobacilli and fungal enzymes called proteases can eliminate gluten and, as a bonus, also reduce the bread's glycemic index — how quickly and how much it raises blood sugar. In contrast, ordinary yeast does not break down gluten and other harmful proteins like gliadin.

Sprouting is also another grain-preparation technique that may reduce the effects of gluten. The basic idea behind sprouting is that as a seed (such as a grain) germinates, it taps into and metabolizes stored carbohydrates to fuel its growth and may partially break down storage proteins such as gluten. Other sources claim that during the sprouting process, gluten gets broken down by the seedling as it taps into the energy contained within the seed's endosperm. Sprouting also releases vitamins, minerals, and other bioactive components that are unavailable for absorption in the unsprouted grain.

So why not just go buy 100% gluten-free bread? Ultimately, gluten-free bread and other gluten-free foods often contain just as many chemicals, preservatives, and sugars as gluten-containing foods, and unless you have a condition such as celiac disease or you are fighting a leaky gut from years of poor eating, you really don't need to avoid gluten entirely. **Instead, I recommend you only eat gluten-containing grains when they are prepared via ancestral processes such as fermentation and sprouting.** Think twice before snagging any old "healthy" goodie from the organic coffee shop, and support your ability to digest gluten by limiting your gut's exposure to chemicals such as pesticides and herbicides. You can also take supplements like Gluten Guardian or gluten polypeptidases to help break down the gluten you do eat. That way, you can have your cake and eat it too, although you still shouldn't turn into a complete breadhead. (Read chapter 13 of my book *Boundless* for more tips on managing gluten and getting a healthy gut.)

In addition to giving you my wife's lovely, world-famous sourdough bread recipe, I'm also going to fill you in on a few other simple methods I use to make bread that doesn't involve any grains or gluten at all.

For all resources, books, tools, and ingredients mentioned throughout this chapter go to: BoundlessCookbook.com/bread

LOW-CARB HIGH-COLLAGEN CHOCOLATE NUT BUTTER LOAF

I first discovered a version of this low-carb, no-grain, protein-packed bread in *Paleo* magazine. It tastes amazingly like bread but with much lower sugar and zero gluten. It's perfect for those who are concerned about gluten.

Total Time

1 hour

Ingredients

4 large eggs

1 teaspoon baking soda

1 cup cashew, almond, or other nut butter*

Tools And Materials

4 × 8-inch loaf pan

Parchment paper

2 heaping scoops of any collagen powder*

½ cup unsweetened or stevia-sweetened dark chocolate chips

*Notes

For the nut butter, I like to use the Artisana brand. I also use Ancient Nutrition's Chocolate Multi-Collagen.

Instructions

1. Preheat the oven to 350 °F. Line the loaf pan with the parchment paper.
2. With a mixer, mix the eggs, baking soda, cashew butter, and collagen until fully combined, then fold in the chocolate chips and spoon the batter into a loaf pan.
3. Bake until golden brown (this takes around 35 minutes) and a toothpick inserted into the center comes out clean.
4. Cool for 15 minutes, then remove, cool on a wire rack completely, and slice.
5. Slathered with a bit of extra nut butter and/or a dollop of yogurt, this "bread" definitely doubles as a dessert.

DR. SARAH MYHILL'S LINSEED LOAF

When I interviewed Dr. Sarah Myhill on my podcast, she shared a bread recipe she gives to her patients with chronic fatigue syndrome, a condition that seems to be particularly aggravated by gluten.

After the podcast, I whipped up a batch of this bread and was surprised at how simple and tasty it turned out, especially when slathered with a big pad of butter. All you need is a blender, an oven, and a few key ingredients. You can use linseed or flaxseed, as the difference between the two is minimal. Linseed is technically a shorter plant with lots of branches and lots of seeds, while flaxseed is taller with fewer branches. Both can prevent constipation, diabetes, high cholesterol, heart disease, cancer, and several other conditions, and contain nutrients including lignans, antioxidants, fiber, protein, and polyunsaturated fatty acids such as alpha-linolenic acid (ALA) and omega-3 fatty acids.

Dr. Myhill recommends using dark or golden linseed grains because the golden grains produce a brown loaf and the dark a black one. Do not use commercially ground linseed as the grinding is not fine enough, and it will have absorbed some water already so this stops it sticking together in the recipe. If you purchase linseed in bulk then you must weigh it really accurately in order to get the proportion of water spot on!

Total Time

1 hour 15 minutes

Ingredients

½ pound whole organic linseed or flaxseed

9½ ounces water

1 heaping tablespoon coconut oil or lard

1 teaspoon of good salt, like Celtic salt

Instructions

1. Preheat the oven to 220 °F.
2. Blend ½ pound whole linseed or flaxseed into a fine flour. This usually takes about 30 seconds. The finer you can grind the flour the better as it sticks together resulting in a firmer loaf. You can do this in two batches because the blender blades tend to "hollow out" the mix so that half does not circulate and grind fully.
3. Pour the ground flour into a mixing bowl. If you do two batches of seeds for better blending, repeat the above with the second half of seeds, and add to the mixing bowl.
4. Add in exactly 9½ ounces water (be precise). Put it all in at once, and do not drizzle it slowly in. Stir it with a wooden spoon. Keep stirring. The mixture will thicken over the course of 30 seconds. Keep stirring until it becomes sticky and holds together in a lump. Initially, it may look as if you have added far too much water! But just keep stirring.
5. Next, use your fingers to scoop up a dollop of coconut oil or lard. Use this to grease the baking tin. Your hands will conveniently now be covered in fat, which means you can pick up your sticky dough without it sticking to your hands.
6. Use your hands to shape the dough until it has a smooth surface. Then drop it into the greased baking tin.
7. Spend about 30 seconds doing this. Do not be tempted to knead or fold the loaf or you will introduce layers of fat that stop it sticking to itself. This prevents the loaf from cracking as it rises and cooks.
8. Let the loaf rest for 5 minutes so it fully absorbs all the water. Meanwhile, you can rub any excess fat into your skin where it will be absorbed as an amazing moisturizer.
9. Put the loaf into the oven at 220 °F for 1 hour.
10. When the timer goes off, take the loaf out of the oven, tip the loaf out of the pan (it should slide out easily), and let it cool on a wire rack.

This bread will stay good in the refrigerator for a week, and also freezes quite nicely.

JESSA GREENFIELD'S WORLD-FAMOUS SOURDOUGH BREAD

Alright, this is officially it: probably the "most-asked-for" recipe the Greenfield family has. My wife Jessa has cracked the code on how to make what I consider to be some of the best sourdough bread I've ever eaten in my life.

The recipe below is written by her with her own personal tips. If you decide to commit to learning a recipe like this, then the pleasurable bread dividends are enormous. But I'll warn you: **this is probably one of the more advanced recipes in this cookbook**, and often involves some trial-and-error to get it exactly right, since room temperatures, atmospheric pressures, humidity, and a host of other factors in your own kitchen environment can slightly change the outcome of the recipe.

Fortunately, sourdough bread has become quite popular in the past decade as people have begun to realize the superior health benefits of fermenting wheat, so the internet now abounds with tips and tricks on sourdough preparation. Hence, a quick internet search can be your friend if you run into trouble or need clarification on any aspects of sourdough starters, sourdough bread preparation, and even more sourdough information. In particular, the book *Sourdough: Recipes for Rustic Fermented Breads, Sweets, Savories, and More* by author Sarah Owens is quite helpful.

Total Time

First rising: 8-12 hours
Second rising: 3-5 hours
Prep and baking: 1 hour 45 minutes

Tools And Materials

Pastry knife

Clay bread pot with a lid

Ingredients

2 cups sourdough starter*

2 cups pure lukewarm water

4 teaspoons salts (this slows down the fermentation process, allowing more good bacteria to grow)

6 cups Einkorn flour (other good alternatives are Himalayan Tartary Buckwheat flour from Angelica Mills — the same HTB you discovered in the introduction to this cookbook — and Molino Grassi Usda Organic Italian Flour, available on Amazon)

*Notes

A sourdough starter is a fermented, two-ingredient mixture of water and flour. You can purchase a done-for-you starter from a good source such as Cultures For Health, or you can make your own. The website FeastingAtHome.com has a perfect recipe for making your own starter, although hundreds of recipes and videos exist to teach you how to make a starter.

Instructions

1. Combine the starter, water, and salt in a large bowl, stir, and let stand for 5 minutes.
2. Start adding flour. Begin with 2 cups of flour, and let it sit for 5 minutes. The reason for this is if you are using whole wheat, it takes time for the water to absorb and many times people end up adding too much flour, making the bread as hard a rock. Next, add another 1 cup flour, and let that then sit for 5 minutes.
3. Continue to add ½ cup at a time so that the bread dough doesn't get too stiff. You want your dough to have the consistency of being able to hold a ball shape that, over time, will flatten.
4. When all flour is added, let your dough sit for 8-12 hours at room temperature. I typically leave it overnight.
5. After the first rise, you need to heavily flour a surface and pour out the dough onto that surface. You should not be able to shape the dough with your hands because it is so sticky. I use a pastry knife to handle the dough and shape the dough into a ball. I recommend you grease your bowl very well and set the dough back into the bowl for the "second rise," which will take 3-5 hours.
6. Just before cooking the bread, you will need to soak a clay pot in water for 30 minutes. This is so that as the bread bakes, it emits steam.
7. Place the pot in an un-preheated oven. Once it is in there, set the oven to its maximum temperature, which is typically around 550 °F.
8. When the oven is preheated to a maximum temperature, take the pot out. Sprinkle cornmeal on the bottom of the pot (this works just like greasing a pan). Loosen the dough from the sides of the bowl with a spatula, and pour it into your clay pot.
9. Put the lid on the pot immediately, and put it back in the oven. Take the temperature down to 450 °F, and cook for 40 minutes. Then remove the lid from the pot, and let the bread cook for another 15 minutes at 350 °F (this will give the crust some good crunch).
10. Take the bread out, and let it cool completely before cutting.

Although it will keep well in a pantry for around 5 days, this bread is best served fresh! Try it with a bit of raw honey and a good salt, dip it in extra virgin olive oil and balsamic vinaigrette, top it with a slathering of nut butter, or use it as the perfect bread for any sandwich, breakfast toast, or dinner side.

SOURDOUGH BREAD

Since you now have a bunch of sourdough starter around from having perfected your bread recipe (right?), you might as well do something else with it that goes beyond bread. My mouth begins to salivate when I'm typing away in my office and smell that my wife has tossed a sourdough pizza in the oven. And although I'm not a big pizza guy, I make a pretty big exception for this variation, especially when finished with a drizzling of olive oil and consumed alongside a big glass of organic red Italian wine.

You'll notice that this recipe calls for "proofing" the sourdough starter. To proof a starter, you take a portion of it out of the refrigerator and feed it for a day or so to get a foamy "proof" that the yeast is active.

Total Time

9 hours 40 minutes

Tools And Materials

Large mixing bowl   Proofing Box

Plastic wrap   Baking sheet

Ingredients

1½ cups sourdough culture   2½ cups water

7 cups unbleached all-purpose or   1½ teaspoons salt
pastry flour*

*Notes

Good flour options include King Arthur Unbleached All-Purpose Flour, Einkorn flour, Himalayan Tartary Buckwheat flour from Angelica Mills, or Molino Grassi Usda Organic Italian Flour.

Instructions

1. Mix together the culture, flour, water, and salt in a large mixing bowl, and knead for at least 30 minutes to develop the gluten.
2. Place the dough in a bowl, cover it with plastic wrap, and proof for 4 hours at 77-82 °F in a proofing box. (These proofing boxes serve as a warming chamber that encourages the fermentation of the dough by the yeast through warm temperatures and controlled humidity.)
3. Punch down and divide into 6 balls, about 8 ounces each. Place the balls on a baking sheet, cover with plastic wrap, and proof for an additional 4 hours at room temperature, or preferably close to 70 °F.
4. To form the pizzas, flatten each round by pressing on the center with the heel of your hand until a ridge begins to form at the periphery. Lift the dough by holding onto the ridge with both hands, and let the weight of the dough stretch the developing circle. Turn the dough to maintain the circle, while alternately pulling on the ridge and pressing on the center until a 10-inch circle is formed with a ¼- inch ridge.
5. Transfer the pizzas to a lightly floured baking sheet or peel and proof for ½-1 hour at room temperature. Sprinkle on the toppings of your choice. Bake in a preheated 500 °F oven, on a preheated stone if you have one, for 7-9 minutes or until the edges begin to brown.

The sky's the limit for your toppings on this pizza, which has the distinctive hearty taste of sourdough with a wonderful combination of crunch and chew on the crust, but a few of my personal favorite toppings are:

- Fig, goat cheese, and arugula
- Avocado and fried egg drizzled with extra virgin olive oil
- Fennel, prosciutto, and pear
- Grilled summer squash with slivered almonds

Hopefully, that gets your creative juices (and Italian saliva) flowing!

08

VEGETABLES

I used to be really, really into eating oodles of vegetables, probably to a fault. From giant handfuls of kale and spinach in a morning smoothie to giant salad bowls overflowing with raw vegetables for my big-ass lunchtime salad, I probably averaged well over 100 grams of fiber a day for years!

However, I eventually realized that "more is not better," and all that excess fiber can actually create gas, bloating, digestive inflammation, and even gut damage due to the hefty amounts of built-in plant defense mechanisms — a topic addressed in detail in Dr. Stephen Gundry's book *The Plant Paradox*. So in the past several years, I've dialed back my vegetable consumption in favor of more nutrient-dense organ meats and superfood smoothies, but certainly still include a decent amount of vegetables in the diet. However, my new approach is — very similar to fermentation of grains — to **cook, soak, sprout, and/or even ferment my vegetables to enhance digestibility, deactivate plant-defense mechanisms, and unlock more nutrients** from my plants.

In addition to a big lunchtime salad comprised of staples such as kimchi, sauerkraut, shoots, microgreens, sprouts, a handful of healthier nuts such as Barùkas or macadamia nuts, and a generous helping of leftover protein from dinner the night before or any fish of the SMASH variety, I also enjoy the recipes I'll share in this section as extra sides with lunch or staples served with dinner.

For all resources, books, tools, and ingredients mentioned throughout this chapter go to:
BoundlessCookbook.com/vegetables

SWEET POTATO
FRIES

These healthy twists on "fries" pair perfectly with the meat dishes in this cookbook, particularly the ribeye steaks or the roast chicken. Baking your fries is much healthier than frying them. It involves slowly cooking your food in the oven with gentle heat. This allows the natural moisture to slowly evaporate, which eliminates the need for added fat and oils.

To bake, all you have to do is season any food and then place it in a pan or dish, covered or uncovered, in the oven. This method also works just fine for any chopped vegetables or root plants, including broccoli, cauliflower, squash, or pumpkin.

Total Time

35 minutes

Ingredients

2 medium to large sweet potatoes

Extra virgin olive oil

Salt

Cayenne pepper

Paprika

Turmeric

Black pepper

Instructions

1. Place the oven rack in the upper third of the oven, and preheat to 425 °F.
2. Spray the baking sheet with non-stick spray.
3. In a large bowl, lightly toss the sweet potatoes and olive oil. Sprinkle with the salt, cayenne pepper, turmeric, black pepper, and paprika.
4. Place the sweet potatoes in a single layer on the baking sheet. Be careful not to overcrowd them.
5. Bake for 18-24 minutes until tender and golden brown, turning occasionally.
6. Cool for 5 minutes before serving.

CARROT FRIES

Limiting your carb intake and feel like sweet potato fries might pack too hefty a starch punch? Or need a creative use for all those extra carrots you might have in the fridge? Look no further. Like sweet potatoes, carrots are a root vegetable but with an even lower sugar content. This alternative fries recipe gives you all the flavor of fries but with relatively fewer carbs.

Total Time

35 minutes

Ingredients

1 pound carrots (about 10 medium carrots) — or more if you'd like leftovers for lunch the next day

2 tablespoons any gluten-free flour, such as coconut, breadfruit, or arrowroot*

2 tablespoons extra virgin olive oil

1 teaspoon good salt

½ teaspoon black pepper

½ teaspoon garlic powder

½ teaspoon onion powder

½ teaspoon thyme

½ teaspoon cayenne, optional

*Notes

The flour is optional, but it can lend some nice added texture and flavor. For an added kick, add the cayenne.

Instructions

1. Preheat the oven to 450 ºF. Wash and peel the carrots, then cut them into even-sized sticks that are roughly 4 inches long and about ½ -inch thick.
2. Put the cut carrots into a large bowl, and sprinkle the flour and all the spices over them until they're thoroughly coated.
3. Drizzle the extra virgin olive oil over the carrots, and stir to evenly coat with oil.
4. Place the carrots on a baking sheet lined with parchment paper. Make sure they are evenly spread and not stacked on top of each other.
5. Place the carrots in the oven, and bake for 20-30 minutes. Check halfway through to move the carrots around or flip them to make sure they cook evenly.
6. The carrots are done when there is a slight browning or crisping on the edges and you can pierce them easily with a fork.
7. Remove them from the oven, and let them cool for a couple of minutes before serving.

I like to dip these bad boys in a generous amount of my secret sauce: Primal Kitchen Ketchup stirred up with Primal Kitchen Mayonnaise in a 1:1 ratio. These also go great with any steak recipe.

FERMENTED
WILD PLANT PESTO

A wild plant is any non-cultivated plant or herb that, when consumed, lends some kind of benefit to your immune system, digestive system, cardiovascular system, or nervous system, or even several of these systems at once. Plants that grow wild are exposed to more environmental stressors than much of the domesticated produce you find in the aisles of the grocery store, and they can pass on their built-in, stress-resilience factors to your body when you consume them. Take mint, for example. The dainty, mild taste of the small mint leaves I can buy in a small plastic container from the grocery store absolutely pales in comparison to the intense flavor and potency of the beat-up wild mint that grows in the forest behind my house — and the latter confers far more benefits.

These "beat-up" fruits and vegetables contain potent compounds that improve your health in a variety of ways, including phenols, polyphenols, phytochemicals, chlorophylls, and cytokines. The scientific term for this is xenohormesis, which simply means that environmentally stressed plants can produce compounds that can confer stress resistance and survival benefits to the animals that consume them. These xenohormetic plant compounds can, when ingested, **improve longevity and fitness** by activating your stress response.

There are thousands of such plants that you can forage and consume. Clover, cattail, chicory, greater burdock, amaranth, field pennycress, plantain, kelp, fireweed, and even the lowly dandelion in your backyard are just a few examples.

One excellent book that explores this topic is *Eating on the Wild Side* by Jo Robinson, which even advises cutting up or tearing apart plants such as kale several hours before eating them. This action causes the plant to believe it is being attacked by a wild animal and to amp up its natural defense mechanisms, which then mildly stress your body upon consumption.

A local wild-plant-foraging class or meetup is a good way to get up to speed on what is growing wild in your area, and a trip to your local farmers market for ugly, dirty, bitter, sour, and misshapen produce can also leave you with a whole canvas bag or burlap sack chock-full of xenohormetic goodies. The trick is to eat as wide a variety of wild plants and herbs as you can by mixing them into teas, smoothies, stir-fries, salads, and other dishes throughout the week. If you are on the go or don't have time to forage, one of my favorite resources for organic, heirloom wild plant extracts and powders is Dr. Thomas Cowan's Vegetable Powders.

By fermenting your plants prior to making the super nutrient-dense wild plant pesto you're about to discover, you amplify the gut-friendly, bacterial content of your pesto, which has a host of antioxidants from the wild plants, with none of the vegetable oils so notoriously found in store-bought pesto. The fermentation also gives the same umami flavor as you'd normally get from parmesan cheese, which is traditionally added to pesto, but without the dairy!

You don't have to use wild plants nor do you necessarily need to ferment your plants prior to making this recipe, but if you do, you'll get far more health benefits and flavor. If you don't ferment and don't mind dairy, just add a ½ cup of grated parmesan cheese to the recipe below.

To ferment, put 8 cups of fresh nettle (this stuff grows like weeds outside my house, and is jam-packed with the nutrients and protein that large animals like deer love to munch on) into a glass Mason jar with 1 teaspoon of salt, and enough water to cover the nettle and 4 ounces of leftover brine from an empty pickle jar. Let it sit on the kitchen counter for 14 days to ferment (nettle takes a bit longer to ferment because it's lower in natural lactobacilli compared to, say, a cucumber for pickles.)

Total Time

10 minutes

Ingredients

2 cups fermented nettle*

¼ cup chopped rosemary (this, the thyme, and the stevia don't have to be wild)

¼ cup chopped thyme

¼ cup chopped stevia leaves or 1 teaspoon stevia or monk fruit powder

2 cups walnuts, raw

1 cup extra virgin olive oil

1 tablespoon sea salt

1 tablespoon ground pepper

Zest of one lemon

*Notes

I also like to include dandelion leaf and wild mint — both of which can be easily grown in a backyard garden or patio, or even harvested in nature if you live near a park or forest! If you don't have fermented nettle, you can use unfermented nettle, and if you don't have that, you can use the "traditional" ingredient of pesto: basil (there's actually no reason you can't toss a little basil into this recipe anyway, which I sometimes do).

Instructions

1. Combine all the ingredients in a food processor and blend.
2. Blend for about 60 seconds, until the texture is thick and clumpy, but not "runny."

That's it! This pesto is amazing slathered over a steak, smeared onto a nori wrap with a bit of sardines and rice, or served over almond or flaxseed crackers.

SPROUTS SNACK MIX

"Sprouts" is a term that refers to a vegetable or plant seed or bean after it begins to germinate. The most common sprouts are alfalfa, soy, and mung bean, as well as a variety of bean sprouts.

Seeds contain a veritable storehouse of all the important nutrients that a plant will need to grow in its early days, so they are filled with important organic compounds, vitamins, and minerals not available to your body in the un-sprouted form.

Sprouts have numerous proven health benefits. They can boost the metabolism, aid the digestive process, boost enzymatic activity, prevent anemia, help with weight loss, lower cholesterol and blood pressure, improve skin health and vision, and support the immune system. They have also been shown to prevent neural tube defects in infants.

I always have a fresh batch of sprouts in the fridge to toss into smoothies or serve over salads and other recipes. But I also often have a glass jar full of salted, low-heat, dehydrated sprouts (high heat can degrade the nutrients in sprouts, so be careful with your dehydrator settings for the recipe below). Consider this to be a process very similar to making chia pets, except with a nutrient and digestibility score that makes sprouts somewhat of a superfood.

Total Time

Prep: 5-8 hours 10 minutes | Sprouting: 3-5 days | "Trail mix:" 12-24 hours

Tools And Materials

Clean measuring cup and spoons

Clean glass jar (a 2-quart jar will give you ample room to grow your sprouts)

Sanitizing agent (Optional, but good for ensuring you kill off any bacteria and limit mold growth. I use 2 tablespoons of 35% food grade hydrogen peroxide or a couple drops grapefruit seed extract essential oil.)

Screen (a dedicated plastic or stainless steel lid fitted with a screen cheesecloth, muslin, or an organic cotton sheet)

Food dehydrator for the "trail mix"

Ingredients

Broccoli and Friends seed mix (this is a perfect, delicious blend of broccoli, red clover, and alfalfa seeds with a high germination rate)

Instructions

1. Inspect your bounty of seeds, and remove any broken, discolored, or damaged seeds.
2. Measure out about ¼ cup of seeds, and put them into your jar.
3. Wash the seeds very thoroughly by gently agitating the jar for about thirty seconds, then straining the water out through the filter on top of the jar.
4. Add enough water to cover the seeds (include a sanitizing agent in your soaking water as an extra precaution), and let soak for 2-3 minutes, then drain.
5. Rinse, cover with fresh water (this time without the sanitizing agent), and let soak for another 2-3 minutes, then drain again.
6. Top your seeds off with water. A ratio of 3:1 water to seeds is a good standard rule. For example, if you are using ¼ cup of seeds, add ¾ cup of water.
7. Soak the seeds for 5-8 hours at room temperature, then drain the water out.
8. Store the jar in a cool, dark place at a 70° angle to ensure that residual water drains out (make sure there's a vessel underneath to catch the water). How do you find a 70° angle? Start with the jar on its side, which is 3 o'clock. Then point the mouth of the jar in the direction of 6 o'clock (90°), but stop a little before so it lands at 5 o'clock (so it's almost upside down but at a slight angle). To achieve that angle, you could set your jar into a sprouting jar stand (you can buy these on Amazon), a bowl, or the groove of a wooden carving board. Anything that will elevate your jar to 70° will work.
9. Rinse and strain the seeds 2 or 3 times a day. Remember that your seeds are alive and fragile. Coddle them. If you shake, squeeze, scrape, or otherwise piss off your budding sprouts, you could crush them or break the sprouts off the seeds prematurely and spoil the bunch.
10. When the tails get about 1-inch long and you start to see leaves forming and splitting, your sprouts are ready to be harvested.
11. Place the jar in a bright part of the room with natural light for a few hours, but not in direct sunlight (direct sunlight will wilt and possibly kill your sprouts), for your sprouts to develop their vibrant green color.
12. Store your sprouts directly in the jar with a standard airtight lid, or transfer them to another container (I keep them in the fridge in a big Pyrex glass container), and refrigerate them for up to 1 week. Rinse them once every 2 or 3 days, and then strain very well to keep them optimally fresh.
13. One last tip for a super nutritious low-calorie "trail mix:" you can put your sprouts into a food dehydrator at 105° for 12-24 hours and sprinkle with a coarse salt like Colima salt. You can then add any other spices you'd like too, such as curry, garlic, cayenne, paprika, cinnamon, etc. I recommend making this one in small batches and keeping it in an airtight container because it only stays crunchy for about 1-2 days.

Everything I know about sprouts, including the recipe above, I learned from *The Sprouts Book* by Doug Evans, so I highly recommend grabbing his book if you want to up your sprouts game, and also learn how to grow even more nutritious goodies from seeds, such as microgreens and shoots!

09

SMOOTHIES

I have always been a fan of smoothies. Perhaps it goes back to my old days as a bodybuilder, during which I'd put toxic, cheap whey protein and a helluva lot of stimulants into a giant shaker cup and down fart-inducing blends throughout an entire day of muscle-building. Or perhaps it's the mad scientist in me that enjoys tossing a bunch of ingredients into a blender and experimenting with the taste and physiology of "what happens next." Or maybe it's just the convenience of not needing to intensively chew and cook.

Either way, for the past couple of decades, my "go-to" breakfast has been some variance of a smoothie. But my own smoothies have a few key important features:

I blend them incredibly thick (we're talking the thickness of ice cream). This is because I find I savor and enjoy my smoothie much better when I slowly eat it with a spoon vs. sucking it down quickly through a straw. There's also a benefit to allowing the digestive enzymes in the mouth to pre-digest the blended goodness prior to swallowing. Admittedly, blending super thick smoothies requires extra stirring and stopping/starting or pulsing your blender during the blending process, but the end, less "liquidy" result is worth it, in my opinion.

I save any crunchy goodies, such as coconut flakes, cacao nibs, bee pollen, spirulina, chlorella, brazil nuts, etc. from the blending step and, instead, sprinkle them on at the end so I get a wonderful texture and crunch while eating my smoothie. Typically I do this by spooning the smoothie with a large spatula into a bowl, then tossing the ingredients on top and mixing them in with my spoon, or — if I'm lazy and don't want to do extra dishes — just stirring them into my blender jar after the blending process and eating my smoothie right out of the blender jar.

I always add a bit of vitamin C (such as a squeeze of half an organic lemon or a teaspoon of any non-GMO ascorbic acid powder) and plenty of ice to my smoothie to prevent excessive oxidation of my spendy superfood ingredients, which can potentially become oxidized from the heat generated by the blender motor and blades.

So I bet you're now wondering what this mysterious smoothie is that I consume each and every morning, refined over the years to a state of near perfection. I'll begin with that recipe, then move on to a few of my other favorite ways to make blended goodness.

For all resources, books, tools, and ingredients mentioned throughout this chapter go to:
BoundlessCookbook.com/smoothies

THE ULTIMATE ANTI-AGING MORNING SMOOTHIE

As I wrote the anti-aging and longevity chapter of my book *Boundless*, which turned out to be the longest chapter of the book by far, I did some pretty intensive research on every last compound that could defy aging, and come up with a full list of everything (and I mean everything) one could easily mix into a morning smoothie with some ice and a liquid of choice (such as bone broth, coconut milk, hemp milk, kefir, etc.) to create the ultimate anti-aging morning breakfast smoothie. We're talking a host of ingredients that target mitochondria, hormesis, inflammation, stem cells, skin/hair/nails quality, NAD and sirtuin pathways, and beyond.

My general approach is to eyeball most of the ingredients you'll find below (although I've given you approximate ballpark amounts I use), blend it all with ice and bone broth to desired texture, top with a superfood like goji berries, dried blueberries, cacao nibs, spirulina, etc. and dig into the culinary nirvana. It is admittedly not a cheap smoothie but you're going to feel like you're 16 years old after you drink this, and have clean energy for hours on end. Bon appetit! At BenGreenfieldFitness.com/antiagingsmoothie, you can find a convenient Amazon list of every single ingredient. You can literally just buy everything off that list and keep in one section of the pantry to quickly add to the blender. You'll also find a list of the ingredients in the resource section (page 169).

The ingredients below will make one giant smoothie or 2 regular sized ones.

Total Time

Prep: 10 minutes

Tools And Materials

Blender

Stirring tamper tool (used to push the food onto the blender)

Large spatula

Ingredients

1 whole avocado for creaminess (an alternative is 4-6 tablespoons coconut cream if you don't like avocados)

2 heaping scoops collagen powder

2 heaping teaspoons organic cacao powder

2 teaspoons organic blueberry powder

2 teaspoons sunflower lecithin (this lends good texture and also increases the bioavailability of all the goodies in the smoothie)

2 teaspoons Ceylon cinnamon

1 teaspoon salt

⅓ tablespoon creatine powder

2 teaspoons of Dr. Cowan's Garden Low Oxalate Greens or a heaping scoop of any other greens powder, such as Organifi or Athletic Greens. For an extra nitric oxide boost, a good beet powder or red powder is also an alternative or addition here, such as Dr. Cowan's Beet Powder or Organifi Red

2 teaspoons Four Sigmatic Ten Mushrooms Blend

continued...

1 packet Four Sigmatic Cordyceps mushroom extract

1 packet Four Sigmatic Lion's Mane mushroom extract

2 teaspoons NOW Foods desiccated liver powder

2 dropperfuls Omica Organics vanilla stevia

1 cup ice (or more for a thicker texture — I like to mix mine thick enough to serve "Açaí bowl" style and eat with a spoon)

Full-fat, organic coconut milk, hemp milk, bone broth, kefir, or any other healthy liquid to desired texture.

Toppings

2-3 tablespoons chlorella or spirulina tablets (I use EnergyBits and/or RecoveryBits)

2-3 tablespoons organic cacao nibs

2-3 tablespoons unsweetened coconut flakes

1 teaspoon good coarse salt

1 teaspoon of Manuka honey

1 teaspoon nut butter

Instructions

1. Blend all smoothie ingredients for 90 seconds to 2 minutes, stirring frequently with the blender stirrer if you're mixing it super thick, like I like to do. Have some of your extra liquid on hand if it's mixing too thick, and extra ice on hand if it's mixing too thin.
2. Use a large spatula to transfer the entire smoothie into a giant mug or bowl.
3. Top with all toppings.
4. Eat with a spoon, savoring every mind-blowing bite.

You can always throw in a few of your other favorite ingredients, too. For example, I'll sometimes toss in a bit of liquid fish oil, C60 oil (listen to my podcast with Ian Mitchell for more on that unique oil), or extra virgin olive oil for added fats, colostrum for extra gut nourishment, or glycine for a bit of added sweetness.

Experiment and enjoy!

AVOCADO
CHOCOLATE PUDDING

This creamy, cocoa-infused treat is one of my favorite low-carb dessert go-to's and is incredibly simple to make. The creaminess of the avocado and coconut milk or coconut cream pairs perfectly with the savory nut butter, and when topped with a few select crunchies. This stuff freezes just fine, so you'll never again have an excuse to be tossing out old leftover rotten and excessively soft avocados. I occasionally even toss in 1 or 2 scoops of a good greens powder to make this into an actual nutrient-dense "meal" option.

Total Time

10 minutes

Tools And Materials

Blender

Ingredients

½ -1 sliced avocado

1 teaspoon cinnamon

1-2 scoops of organic whey or vegan protein

4-6 ounces full-fat, organic coconut milk or coconut cream

1-2 teaspoons almond butter

1-2 teaspoons carob or cocoa powder

A dash of natural vanilla extract or vanilla powder

Unsweetened coconut flakes

Dark chocolate chunks

Instructions

1. Put the sliced avocado in a blender.
2. Add in cinnamon, organic whey or vegan protein, full-fat, organic coconut milk or coconut cream, almond butter, carob or cocoa powder, and a dash of natural vanilla extract or vanilla powder.
3. Blend everything together, and then top with unsweetened coconut flakes or dark chocolate chunks.

Tell me this does not taste like glorious chocolate pudding, and I will call you crazy.

PUMPKIN PIE
SMOOTHIE

If I had to choose a favorite pie, it would probably be good, spicy pumpkin pie with plenty of cinnamon and nutmeg. But pie is time-consuming and messy to make. Why not just take a few ingredients, toss them in a blender, and make yourself a pumpkin pie smoothie? When topped with a good gluten-free granola (there are many options at Thrive Market), you'll swear you're having pie for breakfast, or whenever else you decide to consume this addictively good blend. Who knows? You may even decide to bring it to your next Thanksgiving meal. Your relatives will thank you.

Total Time

10 minutes

Tools And Materials

Blender

Ingredients

1 cup full-fat, organic coconut milk

½ cup organic pumpkin purée

¼ of an avocado

3 tablespoons collagen protein*

1 teaspoon pumpkin pie spice mix and/or Ceylon cinnamon

1 tablespoon maple syrup (or organic vanilla stevia)

½ teaspoon vanilla extract

1 tablespoon of your favorite nut butter

1 tablespoon coconut oil

1 drop Thieves essential oil (optional, but gives a nice added spicy kick)

1 cup ice

*Notes

I recommend Organifi Gold Pumpkin Spice flavor.

Instructions

1. Combine all ingredients in a blender and blend.
2. Add extra milk or ice cubes to reach your desired consistency.

This one is pretty good sprinkled with crumbled pecans and unsweetened coconut flakes. If you're not too concerned about carbs, you can also drizzle it with a touch of Manuka or raw, organic honey for additional flavor bliss.

CARROT CAKE
AÇAÍ BOWL

While pumpkin may be my favorite pie, my favorite cake, by far, is carrot cake. I absolutely love carrot cake, I also like the idea of a big breakfast bowl like an Açaí bowl. But I'm not a huge fan of the massive amounts of sugar both tend to have. Enter my Carrot Cake Açaí bowl, which allows you to have your carrot cake and eat it too, all in the glorious delivery mechanism of an "Açaí bowl"-esque texture.

Total Time

10 minutes

Tools And Materials

Blender

Ingredients (Makes 1 bowl)

2 organic carrots

½ frozen banana

⅓ can full-fat, organic coconut milk

1 tablespoon almond or other nut butter

1 teaspoon cinnamon

1 teaspoon nutmeg

Organic stevia or monk fruit extract to taste

Instructions

1. Add all ingredients. Blend to a thick creamy texture, and add ice if you need to get it even thicker, then use a large spatula to layer in the bottom of a bowl and add the following (optional, but highly recommended) toppings.

Toppings

Gluten-free granola (Thrive Market has plenty of good options)

Unsweetened coconut flakes

Cacao nibs

Chopped macadamia nuts

ELEMENTAL DIET
SMOOTHIE

I often find myself working with clients who have problematic gut issues ranging from small intestine bacterial overgrowth to leaky gut to gastric inflammation — all issues I discuss in detail in Chapter 11 of my book *Boundless*. For these folks, I developed an extremely clean and nourishing smoothie breakfast recipe based on the Elemental Diet.

An Elemental Diet generally consists of no solid meals and instead nutritionally complete formulas in a "pre-digested" form (typically via very expensive canisters of pre-mixed meal formulas in liquid or powder form). Elemental formulas typically contain protein, fat, and carbs that have already been broken down into their building blocks such as amino acids, fatty acids, and sugars, then blended with extra vitamins and minerals. This allows for someone with a compromised gut to get good nutrient density without much "work" for the gut.

Problem is, most Elemental Heal Formulas don't taste that great or, as mentioned above, are quite expensive. So I developed a smoothie recipe that uses smaller amounts of a good Elemental Diet powder formula, then combines it with some key choice ingredients to elevate the taste and offer more calories and nutrient density, since I've found many active athletes and exercise enthusiasts need more calories than is often found in Elemental Diet powdered formulas.

Total Time

10 minutes

Tools And Materials

Blender or shaker cup

Ingredients

1-2 scoops Thorne Mediclear or Dr. Ruscio's Functional Medicine Formulations Elemental Heal Formula*

3⅓ tablespoons non-GMO tapioca, maltodextrin or dextrose (optional, but add these in if you're extremely physically active as these provide additional carbohydrates)

1 high-quality multivitamin, which includes 100% DV of all B vitamins, vitamin C, and vitamin E (I recommend Thorne AM/PM)

1,000 milligrams of L-glutamine powder

1 teaspoon of oil (I recommend coconut oil or extra virgin olive oil)

8 ounces filtered water

Stevia or monk fruit and salt to taste

*Notes

If you can't get this formula, you could substitute in your favorite protein powder or collagen powder. But, it won't be as nutrient-dense or appropriate for the purpose of this smoothie as the Elemental Heal Formula.

Instructions

1. Put all ingredients in a blender or shaker cup, and blend or mix thoroughly.
2. Pour into a glass and enjoy. Like the other smoothie recipes in this cookbook, you can add a bunch of ice and blend it to your preferred thickness, opting to eat with a spoon instead, which is my preferred method.

GO GREENFIELDS BANANA SPICED
OATLESS OATMEAL

My twin boys, world-famous chefs in their own right and hosts of the popular "Go Greenfields" cooking podcast, came up with a gluten-free, gut-friendly "oatmeal" that I personally feel fits quite well into the smoothie section of this cookbook because it's like a giant, warm, spicy smoothie that is absolutely fantastic on a cold winter or fall morning. The main "oat" ingredient in this oatless oatmeal? You guessed it (or maybe not): squash. If you're trying to limit carb intake, you can forego the bananas in the recipe but I think this breakfast tastes much better with the mild sweetness of the banana component.

Total Time

15 minutes

Tools And Materials

Immersion blender

Ingredients

3 cups cooked spaghetti squash

2½ cups canned, full-fat, organic coconut milk

1¼ cups unsweetened, shredded coconut

2 medium-sized, ripe bananas, mashed

2 teaspoons ground cinnamon

¼ teaspoon sea salt

Instructions

1. Combine the squash, coconut milk, coconut, bananas, cinnamon, and salt in a large saute pan or skillet over medium-high heat. Bring to a boil. Reduce the heat to low and simmer, stirring often, for 3-5 minutes.
2. Puree with an immersion blender (a handy kitchen tool that is basically like a tiny, handheld portable blender) to break down the squash a bit, while still leaving some texture. This step is optional, but highly recommended, for the ideal texture.

Serve in big bowls, topped with the shredded coconut, and if desired, a drizzling of organic maple syrup or organic honey.

10

COFFEE AND TEA

Let's face it: there's nothing wrong with a piping hot cup of black coffee or mild, simple mug of green tea. But, **sometimes it's fun and even physiologically helpful to upgrade your coffee or tea with other ingredients**, which I do quite often.

Take coffee blended with fats, for example. When mixed with fats, the cognitively enhancing cholesterols found in the mighty coffee bean (such as cafestol and kahweol) can cross the blood-brain barrier, which they normally wouldn't do, increasing the cognitive benefits of the coffee and extending the mental boost to a level beyond that which caffeine can provide.

In addition, adding fats to coffee can keep you satiated for long periods of time without the hassle of taking time to prepare and eat complicated meals, can boost ketone production (if caprylic acid, MCT, or coconut oil is used as the fat), provide anti-inflammatory, gut-feeding microbiome effects from butyric acid if butter is used, and even provide a slight elevation in metabolic rate due to the thermogenic effect of combining caffeine and any oils that contain medium-chain triglycerides.

Should you be concerned about the added cholesterol from fat in your coffee, you should also know that a good light-medium organic roast is already chock-full of chlorogenic acid, which helps to balance these lipid levels — but if you use a paper filter to make your coffee, you filter out much of the cholesterols anyways (listen to BenGreenfieldFitness.com/412 for a thorough explanation of cholesterols in coffee).

Then there's tea. "Yak butter tea" is an ancient Tibetan recipe that, in Eastern cultures, is considered to bestow greater mind-body balance than simply consuming tea or butter in isolation. The bioavailability of the antioxidants from the catechin compounds in the tea is increased, as is the stimulant methylxanthine in the tea, providing long bouts of focused energy for (if you're Tibetan) grazing, farming, meditating, trekking, or pilgrimages, or (if you're Western) banging out a morning of emails with hyperfocus. The conjugated linoleic acid from butter is the "fat that burns fat" and if you choose to use ghee instead, you can take advantage of many of the anti-inflammatory and anti-carcinogenic compounds of that wonderful fat.

Of course, if you're blending an appreciable amount of calories into your coffee or tea, please do understand that these "count" toward your total calorie allotment for the day, and sucking down 400-600 calories of fat with your coffee or tea in most cases count as your breakfast — so I don't recommend consuming any of these more calorie-dense recipes with a mess of scrambled eggs or a breakfast burrito. Deal? OK, here are a few of my favorite recipes.

For all resources, books, tools, and ingredients mentioned throughout this chapter go to: BoundlessCookbook.com/coffeetea

CACAO-CHAGA
SIPPING CHOCOLATE

MiCacao — one of my favorite coffee alternatives — is a concentrated mix of cacao nibs and cacao shells that gives you the experience of drinking pure chocolate but with zero calories.

For this recipe, I prepare it in a French Press by pouring hot water over the 4-6 tablespoons of the MiCacao, then letting it steep for 5-10 minutes. When blended with immune-boosting Chaga extract and mind-boosting Lion's Mane extract, a bit of coconut oil, ghee, or other fat of choice, and high-quality stevia, your brain will be fired up for hours, and you'll have quite happy taste buds to boot. Because the melanin from Chaga can interact with light to help produce ATP (even in the absence of calories — a concept known as "human photobiomodulation"), this is a perfect drink before a morning or afternoon sunshine walk, infrared sauna treatment, the use of a photobiomodulation panel such as JOOVV, or any other exposure to photons of light.

Total Time

5 minutes

Tools And Materials

French Press

Nutribullet or heat-friendly blender

Ingredients

12-24 ounces (depending on how much you want to drink) of MiCacao tea. For an added caffeine boost, I'll occasionally use half-MiCacao and half-coffee.

2 packets Four Sigmatic Chaga mushroom extract

2 packets Four Sigmatic Lion's Mane extract

1 dropperful Omica Organics butterscotch toffee or vanilla stevia

1 teaspoon of a good salt

1-3 tablespoons (depending on how much of an appetite-satiating effect you desire) of ghee, butter or coconut oil, or 1-2 teaspoons of MCT oil or caprylic acid (the latter is a particularly potent source of brain-boosting ketones, but can be more expensive)

Instructions

1. Into a Nutribullet or any other heat-friendly blender, put in all the ingredients.
2. Blend on high for about 90 seconds, then open your blender carefully as contents can expand and get foamy (and the foam is oh-so-delicious).
3. Finally, there are a variety of twists on this recipe. For example, you can just blend hot water, Chaga, stevia, and ghee for simplicity (which I often do), or just blend coffee, Lion's Mane, stevia, and coconut oil for another energetic variant. Feel free to use your creativity!

REISHI RELAXATION TEA

This is perfect before an afternoon nap, as reishi mushroom extract is incredibly relaxing but won't leave you waking groggy or excessively tired. The recipe is simple: pour hot water over 2 packets of Four Sigmatic Reishi. Similar to the Chaga recipe above, you then blend with stevia and ghee (or coconut oil or any other fat) for more flavor, texture, and absorbability. My own favorite method? Simple: reishi, stevia, and ghee.

BLACK PEPPER TEA

This one is quite simple, and a trick I learned when I was reading my friend Emily Fletcher's new book *Stress Less, Accomplish More*. In it, I came across the concept that black pepper tea is an Ayurvedic technique used to significantly heat and warm the body, and can even induce a mild fever. So I thought... what the heck... why not try this stuff before a sauna session? I ground 10 turns of black pepper from my pepper grinder into a mug, added hot water, drank the tea, and then hit the sauna. I'm nearly positive this was not a placebo effect, but the sauna seemed far hotter, along with my sweat rate.

The recipe is simple: 1 teaspoon-ish of black pepper added to hot water. To kick it up a notch, add a pinch of cayenne pepper, and any other Indian warming spices, such as coriander, cumin, mustard powder, paprika, or ginger.

NIGHTTIME AUTOPHAGY TEA

This "autophagy tea" was introduced to me by my friend Dr. Joseph Mercola, who studied up on all the compounds one could drink at night to upregulate the production of NAD — a potent anti-aging compound — and also maximize autophagy, the body's natural cellular clean-up process that is normally triggered by extensive fasting but can also be activated by the specific ingredients in this tea. I simply order them all in bulk powder, put them all together in proper ratios in a glass Mason jar so I don't have to make a new batch every night, then mix with warm or hot water or yogurt at night (best to consume at night prior to the beginning of an overnight intermittent fast).

Ingredients

1 teaspoon Pau d'Arco powdered tea

½ teaspoon hydroxycitrate and garcinia (HCA/Garcinia powder)

½ teaspoon quercetin powder

½ teaspoon glycine powder

½ teaspoon chamomile powder

Lakanto monk fruit sweetener to taste

11

BROTHS

A basic bone broth is made by simmering the bones and connective tissue of animals.You can use the bones from almost any animal (such as pork, beef, veal, turkey, bison, buffalo, chicken, fish, lamb, or venison) to make bone broth. You can also use marrow and connective tissues such as feet, beaks, hooves, gizzards, or fins. (Though I don't condone the environmental sustainability of using creatures such as sharks and turtles in your bone broth.)

In the culinary arts, bone broth is well-known as a highly nutritious "broth" commonly used in soups, sauces, and gravies. But in recent times, it has gained popularity as a health tonic, and for good reason.

For example, **bone broth is fantastic for your gut.** This is because of its relatively high collagen content, which forms gelatin during the bone broth preparation process. Collagen and gelatin contain high amounts of the amino acids glutamine and proline, which are very nourishing to the digestive system and also support a healthy inflammatory response. The nutrients hyaluronic acid, glucosamine, chondroitin, calcium, and magnesium in bone broth all support joint mobility and healthy inflammatory response amino acids like glycine and proline.

Collagen is very popular in the beauty industry and is used in moisturizers, face creams, and serums. The problem is, the collagen molecules are too big to be absorbed through the skin. But that same collagen is very bioabsorbable when consumed via drinking bone broth. The glycine in bone broth can not only balance out the high amounts of methionine you get from eating muscle meat but is also wonderful for supporting sleep quality (see my glycine-rich Bedtime Jello recipe on page 134), especially when paired with the minerals in bone broth such as calcium and magnesium.

Should you not have the time to prepare your own broth, I would encourage you to look into the company Kettle & Fire. This is a packaged done-for-you bone broth made with grass-fed bones. They slowly simmer grass-fed beef bones or organic chicken bones for up to 24 hours, which allows ample time for the nutrients, collagen, and amino acids to soak into the broth. They source all their bones from farms who raise their animals without any added hormones or antibiotics, and their packaging is made from natural and renewable materials. For these reasons, if you're going to skip the step of preparing your own bone broth, then I think Kettle & Fire is a superior alternative to most store-bought bone broths.

The process of making bone broth is quite simple: you take your bones and bits of an animal, along with any spices and vegetables of choice, toss it all into a slow cooker, and let it simmer in liquids such as filtered water, vinegar, and lemon juice (or if you're like me, even a few splashes of leftover beer or wine) for about a day or so. Recipes on the internet abound, so I'll forego painstakingly giving you bone broth preparation instructions, and instead focus on two ways that I personally enjoy a good bone broth.

For all resources, books, tools, and ingredients mentioned throughout this chapter go to: BoundlessCookbook.com/broths

DR. THOMAS COWAN'S BONE BROTH BREAKFAST

Dr. Thomas Cowan, a very popular repeat podcast guest of mine, consumes this highly nutritious recipe for breakfast every morning. While it may not be enough calories for a big breakfast enthusiast, it can easily be paired with a mess of scrambled eggs or breakfast sausages for a full meal. You've already learned why I often use his organic, heirloom wild plant extracts and powders, and they're a key staple of this recipe (although you could easily use your own organic herbs and spices if you prefer).

Total Time

10 minutes

Ingredients

1 cup bone broth

1 teaspoon of any two Thomas Cowan's vegetable powders (ashitaba, three-fold blend savory, three-fold blend slightly sweet, low oxalate greens and sea vegetables, etc.)

2-3 tablespoons sauerkraut

1 packet Miracle Noodle capellini or Angel Hair shirataki noodle pasta

Cayenne pepper, to taste

Instructions

1. To a giant cup of piping hot bone broth, add a heaping 1 teaspoon of any of 2-5 of Thomas Cowan's vegetable powders (my favorite are Ashitaba, Low Oxalate Greens, and Sea Vegetables).
2. After transferring to a bowl, add a big dollop of sauerkraut and consume like soup.
3. One twist I've used for this recipe is to wash, rinse, and add a packet of Miracle Noodle Capellini or Angel Hair shirataki noodle pasta, which basically turns this soup into a superfood version of Top Ramen. I also like to add a bit of cayenne pepper for an additional kick.

BEN'S THANKSGIVING LEFTOVERS BONE BROTH KITCHEN SINK RECIPE

If there's one thing I try to avoid, it's food waste. Of course, Thanksgiving meals can be rife with tons of food getting tossed into the trash. So each year, I instead gather all the leftovers and make a giant pot of what I call my "Kitchen Sink" bone broth, since it really does use just about every ingredient I can find after the Thanksgiving meal.

This is another one of those recipes that, like stone soup, doesn't have a specific ratio, amount, or type of ingredients, but upon reviewing how I personally throw it together, hopefully, you come away with a good approximation of how it's done. The finished product will not taste acidic. Feel free to add other aromatics of your choice, such as parsley, leeks, and peppercorns. I keep a ziplock bag of accumulated food scraps like parsley stems or fennel tops in my freezer for soup and broth.

Total Time

6 hours 10 minutes to 24 hours

Tools And Materials

Slow cooker

Ingredients

1 roasted turkey carcass, along with as many of the leftover, gnawed-upon turkey bones you can hunt down or gather off people's leftover plates (don't worry, a piping hot 24 hours in the slow cooker does a good job killing germs)

1 large carrot, roughly chopped

1 onion, roughly chopped

2 celery stalks, roughly chopped

3 bay leaves

3 garlic cloves

2 large thyme sprigs

3 quarts or so of filtered water

¼ cup apple cider vinegar (the apple cider vinegar helps to extract minerals from the bones while adding a good depth of flavor to the broth)

A splash of any leftover beer or wine from the Thanksgiving meal

Instructions

1. Add all ingredients into a large slow cooker.
2. Bring to a boil on high, and then simmer on low for anywhere from 6 hours up to a day or longer. (You'll find the flavor "evolves" in a quite satisfactory way the longer you simmer, and I'll often return to the slow cooker for up to 2 days for generous helpings of this tasty brew, which also makes the house smell absolutely fantastic.)
3. You can store any leftovers in a large glass Mason jar in the fridge or freeze in a BPA-free, freezer-safe container.

12

FERMENTS

From fermented wild-plant pesto (page 89) to sourdough bread (page 77), you've already discovered plenty of fermented recipes in this cookbook. So what is fermentation exactly? Simply put, it is a process that involves the breakdown of sugars by bacteria and yeast. It is an ancient practice for preserving food and changing or boosting the flavor of food, and it also has a host of other benefits, including **enhancing nutrient and protein availability, digestibility, enzyme availability, and beneficial bacterial content** of a food. Should fermentation sound intimidating or scary to you, consider an extremely basic, simple sauerkraut recipe as a perfect way to see the ease of fermentation.

For simple sauerkraut, you just put a bunch of shredded cabbage into a clean, sanitized tub or bowl. Add a few tablespoons of salt, then massage the cabbage and salt for 5 minutes or so with clean hands. A bit of liquid will begin to form, and this is called the "brine." Transfer the cabbage, salt, and brine to a large glass Mason jar, add a few more tablespoons of saltwater, then press down on the cabbage to mash it down into the jar as far as possible. Cover the mouth of the mason jar with a cloth and secure it with a rubber band or twine. Then, let it ferment for a few days on your countertop. Granted, this is an extremely simple explanation of sauerkraut and you can find plenty tastier, more thorough recipes online, but hopefully, this example helps you realize how simple it is to unlock nutrients and create new flavors in food by letting bacteria do much of the hard work for you.

The Art of Fermentation by Sandor Katz is my favorite comprehensive resource on fermentation in general, fermentation recipes, and fermentation health benefits. Before I give you a few of my favorite fermentation recipes, there are two common questions I'm often asked about fermentation that I'll quickly address.

First, why not just take a probiotic? While I'm a fan of supplementing with a good probiotic capsule, especially when, say, you're coming off a hefty antibiotic regimen and need to introduce specifically selected bacteria in a capsule, or you're traveling and can't hunt down high-quality fermented foods, I'm convinced that bacteria-rich fermented foods themselves offer a distinct advantage over probiotic supplementation. Why? Two reasons, really.

First, many fermented foods, such as kimchi and sauerkraut, contain significant amounts of fiber. This fiber serves as a prebiotic-rich source of food for the bacteria and can increase their survival time and proliferation capability within the gut. Even lower fiber fermented foods such as yogurt and kefir can elevate levels of beneficial bacteria such as Bifidobacteria and Lactobacilli bacteria — all the way down to your colon! It's quite seldom that a probiotic capsule, if it even survives the acidic nature of the gut, can achieve the same depth and amount of bacterial seeding as a wide variety of fermented foods.

Next, if you think about a large bolus of fermented food traveling through your digestive tract, then you can imagine that food essentially "painting" the entire interior of your gut with nourishing bacteria — versus a probiotic capsule, which "sprinkles" bacteria here and there throughout the gut, but may simply not be as thorough a method of populating the gut as fermented foods.

Second, can't you get sick from bacteria produced during home fermentation? It is true that when you're leaving bacteria-rich food out on your kitchen counter, or in a yogurt maker, or an oven, or a food dehydrator, you do increase the chances of pathogenic contamination, this is far less likely to occur if you pay attention to proper sanitation and sterilization practices when fermenting.

Sanitation involves cleaning all your fermentation tools very well, which means wiping down with soap and water and thoroughly rinsing all your fermentation jars, spoons, lids, etc. Sterilization involves killing any bacteria, virus, or fungus by boiling these same materials prior to making a ferment with them. I think both steps are important and advisable if you want to be completely safe with your fermentation practice. So, if you sanitize and sterilize, then fermentation is a completely safe practice.

For all resources, books, tools, and ingredients mentioned throughout this chapter go to: BoundlessCookbook.com/ferments

CREAMY, CREAMY KEFIR

I find kefir to be absolutely fascinating and personally use it not only as a probiotic-rich health tonic drink but also as a base for smoothies (instead of, say, coconut or almond milk or bone broth) and also as a marinade for meats, for which it works surprisingly well. Kefir is basically a cultured, fermented beverage that tastes a bit like drinking yogurt, or slightly tart, creamy milk. Just like sourdough is made using a starter, kefir is made using a starter "grain," which is a combination of yeasts, milk proteins, and bacteria. Kefir originated in Eastern Europe and Russia, where it is traditionally prepared by inoculating cow, goat, or sheep milk with kefir grains.

These grains are living microorganisms that aren't a grain like rice, wheat, or barley but technically a gelatinous polysaccharide culture of bacteria and yeast. The beverage seems to have first come into popularity in the Caucasus Mountains, where the nomadic Ossetians experimented with adding kefir grains to goatskin bags, then letting the grains ferment into a diluted, milk-like drink they would drink for days on end for sustained, healthy energy.

The basic concept of kefir is quite simple: you buy kefir grains (I get mine from Cultures For Health), then grow them in milk (I use goat's milk), which takes about 24 hours every time you make a new batch. You can use the grains over and over again for new batches of kefir, and, just like the "mother" used to make the fermented drink kombucha, the grains eventually flourish and grow, and can be given away to friends or family to begin to make their own kefir, making this drink a gift that keeps on giving!

Here's my own kefir recipe, adapted from my friends at Cultures For Health.

Total Time

24 hours

Tools And Materials

A glass jar

A non-metal stirring utensil

A breathable cover for the jar such as a tight-weave towel, butter muslin, paper towel, or paper coffee filter

A band to secure the cover to the jar like a rubber band or canning jar ring

A fine mesh plastic strainer for removing the kefir grains from the finished kefir

Ingredients

1-2 teaspoons kefir grains

2-4 cups organic cow or goats milk*

*Notes

The amount of milk you use is up to you, but I find that I tend to drink about 4 cups a week, so this amount works perfectly.

Instructions

1. Transfer the active kefir grains into up to 4 cups of fresh milk.
2. Cover with a coffee filter or butter muslin secured by a rubber band or jar ring.
3. Place in a warm spot, 68-85 °F, to culture.
4. Culture until the milk is slightly thickened and the aroma is pleasant. This generally takes 24 hours but can take less time in warmer temperatures, so keep an eye on your grains.
5. After the milk changes the texture and culturing is complete, separate the kefir grains from the finished kefir.
6. Place the kefir grains in a new batch of milk.
7. Store the finished kefir in the refrigerator.

Once I finish making my kefir, I add a scoop of Kion colostrum and a scoop of a good prebiotic fiber mix to the strained kefir jar that I've poured my prepared kefir into (I use acacia fiber powder or ATPScience's "GutRight" formula, although any prebiotic powder formula will do). These additions seem to allow for a far more rich and creamy kefir, as they can help to feed and stabilize the bacteria. When I do this, I strain my first kefir into a glass Mason jar and then leave on the counter for an extra 6-8 hours with the prebiotics and colostrum to concentrate even more bacteria via what is called "secondary fermentation." This step basically supercharges and upgrades your kefir!

If after making kefir for a while, you decide you don't need 4 cups every day, you can absolutely make smaller batches. If you ever reach a point where you need or want to take a break from making milk kefir (such as a 2-week vacation during which you can't care for your precious kefir), there are a few ways you can put your kefir grains on pause. This includes refrigerating them in a small amount of milk for shorter breaks or drying them for longer breaks. In either case, it's important that your grains have been activated and that you have cultured kefir regularly for 3-4 weeks before you attempt either of these resting methods. I highly recommend the Cultures For Health website to learn even more kefir tips and tricks, or to buy your kefir supplies.

COLLAGEN COCONUT
YOGURT

Dr. William Davis, a leading cardiologist and the author of the brilliant book, *Undoctored*, first introduced me to this special yogurt that heals the gut, shuts down appetite, increases collagen production for hair, skin, and nail quality, and even enhances the production of the trust and love hormone oxytocin. No joke. The stuff is super simple to make at home, and I often whip up big batches of this yogurt for smoothies, salad dressing, or just a treat all by itself. I personally modify Dr. Davis's original recipe and add gelatin and vanilla stevia after making it, then refrigerate for an awesome creamy treat. The yogurt uses a specific strain of bacteria, produced by the Swedish company BioGaia, called "Lactobacillus reuteri ATCC PTA 6475." One other unique probiotic to use for this recipe is Mutaflor, especially good for constipation.

Based on studies conducted at MIT and elsewhere, both experimental animal and human, the effects of this particular bacterial strain include complete shut-down of appetite cravings, a dramatic increase in skin thickness and skin collagen, along with the acceleration of skin healing, a doubling of oxytocin blood levels, reduced insulin resistance, increases in testosterone in males, increased estrogen in females, and even thicker and more plentiful hair. Other studies have demonstrated substantial weight loss, particularly from visceral fat, increased muscle mass, and increased bone density. Wow! The problem is in BioGaia's supplement, there are only 100 million CFUs (live organisms) per tablet. But you can significantly amplify these bacterial counts by adding prebiotic fibers and fermenting the capsules into yogurt.

Total Time

48 hours

Tools And Materials

Food dehydrator

Ingredients

2 cans full-fat, organic coconut milk

Omica Organics vanilla or butterscotch toffee stevia (I use 6 dropperfuls)

4 heaping scoops Great Lakes Powdered Gelatin

10 BioGaia Gastrus L-Reuteri probiotic capsules, broken open into

a bowl, or if in tablet form, ground into a fine powder with a mortar and pestle

2 scoops acacia fiber or any other prebiotic fiber blend

1 tablespoon cane sugar to help feed the bacteria

Instructions

1. Mix all ingredients well in a clean stainless steel or ceramic bowl, then leave in a food dehydrator, oven, or yogurt maker at 115 °F for 24 hours.
2. Refrigerate for 1 day.
3. You will have a jello-like texture if done properly. This yogurt is also absolutely fantastic when drizzled with a bit of raw honey and nut butter for a healthy dessert.

IMMORTALITY
YOGURT

In a podcast episode about fringe biohacks nobody's heard of (BenGreenfieldFitness.com/FringeBiohacks), my guest talked about a probiotic capsule that contained a bacterial strain he referred to as "Immortalis" due to the fact that the bacteria were combined with a protein that is often hailed as the Holy Grail of longevity: the Klotho protein.

Your body's circulating levels of Klotho protein decrease with age, and the Klotho gene is associated with an increased risk of nearly every age-related disease. The way my guest explained it is that Klotho proteins actually alter the gravitational pull inside cells, thus changing the time perspective in which those cells can heal (e.g. 40 hrs of healing within a 24 hr time frame). By doing so, the DNA in your cells actually age slower. I know this sounds crazy, but do a Pubmed search for "Klotho protein" and you'll find some pretty compelling research backing up this idea.

So Klotho proteins have major effects on enhancing longevity but they cannot simply be consumed exogenously like a steak, and instead must be combined with a blend of probiotic precursors to have the so called "immortality" effect. The best way to multiply by over a hundred-fold the effects of these probiotics is to ferment them with Klotho protein in yogurt. Problem is, the only company that sells the Immortalis Klotho Formula — which you can find at BenGreenfieldFitness.com/klotho — sells it for about $750 for one bottle, which is approximately a one month supply.

Granted, by making yogurt out of the bottle, you can get more benefits from the capsules and also extend your bottle life significantly, out to approximately 3 months. Think about it this way: if you use a good countertop yogurt maker with 7 tiny glass jars (the one I use is in the resource section for this cookbook) and are using 2 capsules per jar, then, like I do, taking 2 weeks to consume all 7 servings of yogurt, you're only using 14 capsules every 2 weeks. Roughly, this means a bottle that is supposed to last you a month instead lasts you 3 months, which is obviously pretty significant if you're paying that much money for a probiotic. Don't have the budget for Klotho? The good news is that the strategy you're about to learn will greatly increase the number of bacteria of pretty much any probiotic formula you decide to use.

So if you are A) bored and B) have money burning a hole in your pocket for expensive anti-aging probiotics, then try this recipe out. As an added bonus, this yogurt tastes amazing (heck, it better for that price) and is incredibly nourishing to the gut.

BEDTIME JELLO

During a fascinating dinnertime discussion with my friends and brilliant biohackers Ron Penna and Joel Greene, I learned that gelatin (yes, the same stuff you find in J-E-L-L-O) is a rich source of glycine, an amino acid with a mildly sweet taste that helps your body make serotonin, a hormone, and neurotransmitter that has significant effects on sleep and mood, along with a significant appetite-satiating effect. After that discussion, I began making my own jello for pennies on the dollar (while avoiding the artificial colors and sweeteners of the store-bought stuff), and found it to be an incredibly effective nighttime, low-calorie dessert for satiating appetite and improving sleep.

Total Time

2 hours 10 minutes

Tools And Materials

Small saucepan

8 x 8-inch square baking dish.

Ingredients

4 cups fresh-squeezed fruit juice or coconut water*

3 tablespoons raw honey*

3 tablespoons grass-fed gelatin powder (add more if you like your jello super firm, which I do)

*Notes

I use coconut water and have even experimented with full-fat, organic coconut milk for a bit more creamy and slightly higher calorie jello.

The honey is optional, but it seems to also help quite a bit with sleep, likely due to the slow bleed of carbohydrates into your system while you're sleeping.

Instructions

1. Pour the juice or coconut water in a medium-sized small saucepan.
2. Sprinkle gelatin powder over the liquid, and stir it in well.
3. Turn the heat on medium low, and bring the liquid to a simmer, stirring occasionally until the gelatin is dissolved. This should take 5-10 minutes.
4. Turn off the heat, and add the honey if using.
5. Pour into an 8 x 8-inch square baking dish.
6. Refrigerate until the jello is set, about 2 hours.

I eat about a 2 x 2-inch square before bed. That may seem small, but that's all it seems to take for the potent appetite-satiating and sleep-enhancing effects! For more scientific details and to read up on why this trick works so well for sleep, I highly recommend you grab and read Joel Greene's book, *The Immunity Code*.

13

DESSERT

Wait. Dessert in a healthy cookbook? Absolutely! The fact is, I eat dessert just about every evening of the week. However, I save all my carbohydrate intake for the end of the day, which keeps my body in fat-burning mode all day long, then, at some point prior to dinner, I do some kind of strength training or high-intensity interval training and/or a cold soak or cold shower.

Either of these methods shifts your body into a state of insulin sensitivity and up-regulates glucose transporters, ensuring that any sugars you consume afterward don't spend much time in the bloodstream, and are more readily partitioned into your muscle and liver tissue as storage glycogen, especially if those muscle and liver glycogen stores are somewhat empty because you haven't eaten carbs all day. I'll often also, prior to my evening carbohydrate refeed, consume some type of herb or spice that further enhances insulin sensitivity, such as berberine, bitter melon extract, Ceylon cinnamon, apple cider vinegar, or even any of the bitters rich cocktails you'll find in the cocktail section of this cookbook on page 155.

So yes, with these strategies, you can "have your cake and eat it too:" save all carbs for the end of the day, exercise and/or do cold thermogenesis prior to dinner, and consume compounds prior to dinner that shifts your body into a more insulin sensitive state.

For all resources, books, tools, and ingredients mentioned throughout this chapter go to: BoundlessCookbook.com/dessert

BARÙKAS NUT
CHEESECAKE

If your idea of cheesecake is a giant slice of sugar and engineered fats from The Cheesecake Factory, then you're missing out on the experience of a truly healthy, guilt-free slice of heaven. Turns out that — despite always being somewhat calorie dense — cheesecake can indeed be healthy. However, in most cases, there's not going to actually be any true dairy cheese in it if so. Enter nuts! When you soak nuts for anywhere from 2-8 hours (preferably rinsing them a few times during that soaking process to enhance digestibility and eliminate or reduce enzyme inhibitors), the end result is a perfect medium to toss into a blender for a nut "cheese" that can then be used as a cheesecake filler. (Alternatively, you can simply stir a few choice herbs and spices into such a nut cheese for an amazing cracker and vegetable dip!)

Anyway, this Barùkas Nut Cheesecake is in no way a sugar bomb, and it's also incredibly nutritious. In addition, the blueberry powder not only lends the cheesecake a dark, rich blue hue, but also gives you a huge punch of DNA-repairing sirtuins. I like to make this cheesecake and keep it in the refrigerator for a dessert, or even as a tasty treat I can chop up and add as a topping to any of my smoothies or yogurts.

Total Time

4 hours 45 minutes

Tools And Materials

7-inch Cheesecake mold pan

Blender

Crust

½ cup coconut oil

½ cup shredded coconut

1 cup coconut or other gluten-free flour

½ cup ground flax seeds

1 teaspoon vanilla extract

Stevia or monk fruit to taste

Sea salt to taste

Filling

1½ cups soaked, peeled Barùkas*

1½ cups soaked cashews

Juice of 2 lemons

¼ teaspoon lemon zest

1 cup organic blueberry powder

½ cup melted coconut oil

Stevia or monk fruit to taste

Sea salt to taste

Topping

3 tablespoons cashew or other nut butter

1 teaspoon MCT Oil

1 teaspoon almond or full-fat, organic coconut milk

1 teaspoon organic blueberry powder

Stevia or monk fruit to taste

Goji berries and coconut flakes for "texture"

*Notes

If you don't have Barùkas, you can also use macadamia nuts.

Generally, soak Barùkas for about 4 hours and rinse 1-2 times during that soak. The peeling process is optional but can give your cheesecake a smoother texture.

Instructions

1. Mix all crust ingredients in a mixing bowl, and massage with your hands until thoroughly mixed.
2. Into a cheesecake mold pan, place the crust mixture, and use your hands to mold it into the dish, pressing firmly on all edges. Once it's nicely molded, place the crust in the freezer for about 10 minutes until it hardens.
3. While the crust cools, in a high-speed blender, place all ingredients for the filling. Blend at low speed and increase it to high until it becomes a soft mixture. Taste it, and if you want more acidity, you can add more lemon.
4. Place the filling mixture on top of your hardened crust, and spread it evenly with a large spatula.
5. With a spoon or fork, mix all topping ingredients, except the Goji berries and coconut flakes, into a bowl, then drizzle the topping over the surface of the cheesecake. This part is a bit like making art: I like to pour everything from the topping bowl slowly over the surface of the cheesecake, then dress it up nicely by sprinkling the Goji berries and coconut flakes over the topping.
6. Place in the freezer for 20 minutes, then switch to the fridge to chill for 4 hours or overnight.
7. Once the filling is hardened with the consistency of cheesecake and it's nice and cold, it's ready to devour!

BARÙKAS CHOCOLATE-VANILLA NUT BUTTER

What you're about to learn how to make is the most addictively rich and delicious nut butter I've ever shoved into my gaping maw. While you can use just about any nut you desire to whip up this easy nut butter recipe (or the previous cheesecake recipe), my personal favorite nut is the mighty Barùkas nut.

This Amazonian superfood nut is jam-packed with protein, fiber, omega-3 fatty acids, and antioxidant power, with fewer fat calories than any other nut. On my website, you can listen to 2 podcast interviews with the "Superfood Hunter" Darin Olien, in which we discuss how he first discovered this nut, and the variety of health benefits it bestows.

Total Time

15 minutes

Tools And Materials

Food processor

Ingredients

2 cups Barùkas Nuts (soaked almonds, macadamia nuts or cashews — or a mix of nuts — also work well if you don't have Barùkas nuts)

¼ cup melted coconut oil

1 teaspoon vanilla extract or vanilla powder

3 teaspoons cacao extract

½ teaspoon cinnamon

Sea salt, stevia, or monk fruit flavoring to desired taste

Instructions

1. Place the Barùkas Nuts in a food processor for 5-10 minutes, breaking up the mass and scraping down the sides of the processor as needed.
2. Add half of your ¼ cup of coconut oil, and continue to process.
3. Once your mix is more of a butter consistency, add the vanilla, cacao, cinnamon, any additional spices or flavorings you desire, along with remaining oil, and pulse until smooth.

I actually like to keep this nut butter in the fridge so it stays very firm, and cut off little pieces of it for toppings on smoothies or yogurts.

PALEO PUMPKIN DONUTS

Healthy donuts? You bet. These mouth-watering treats are the brainchild of my little kitchen wizards River and Terran Greenfield, who are big fans of baked goodies, and increasingly seem to be cracking the code on how to make traditionally unhealthy breakfast foods or desserts be both healthy and flavorful. These donuts, in my opinion, are absolutely amazing when dipped in a piping hot cup of black coffee.

Total Time

30 minutes

Tools And Materials

Blender

Donut molds

Piping bag

Ingredients

¼ cup butter

3 tablespoons honey

2 eggs

¼ cup milk (organic goat, cow, or coconut milk)

½ cup pumpkin purée

2 teaspoons vanilla

2 cups almond flour

4 tablespoons bone broth protein powder

2 teaspoon pumpkin pie spice

1 teaspoon baking soda

Instructions

1. Preheat the oven to 375 °F, then melt butter and honey together. Whisk the eggs, milk, pumpkin puree, and vanilla. Then add the butter and honey mixture, and mix well. In another bowl, mix all dry ingredients.
2. Pour wet ingredients into the dry ingredients one cup at a time to avoid lumps. Fill piping with batter, and pipe into donut molds.
3. Bake on the top rack for 10-15 minutes.

PUMPKIN CUSTARD

Have some leftover pumpkin puree from the doughnut recipe above, or want a super easy custard you can whip up in no time flat? Here's yet another wonderful dessert recipe courtesy of my sons' GoGreenfields cooking podcast.

Total Time

2 hours 40 minutes

Tools And Materials

Saucepan

Medium bowl

Ramekins

13 x 9-inch baking pan

Ingredients

1 can pumpkin purée

2 egg yolks

2 whole eggs

1 teaspoon vanilla extract

1 cup organic heavy cream or full-fat, organic coconut milk or coconut cream

¼ cup honey

4 packs stevia

2 teaspoons pumpkin pie spice (Primal Palate and Ava Jane's Kitchen both have good options for this)

½ teaspoon of a good salt like Celtic sea salt

Instructions

1. Preheat the oven to 350 °F. On a stovetop, combine the pumpkin puree and cream or coconut milk into a saucepan. Heat until just the cream boils.
2. Meanwhile, in a medium bowl combine combine the eggs, egg yolks, vanilla, honey, stevia, pumpkin spice, and salt.
3. Mix well, then pour the pumpkin/cream mixture into the egg mixture slowly while stirring the egg mixture quickly.
4. Pour into individual ramekins (tiny baking dishes perfectly sized for a dish like custard), and then place the ramekins into a 13 x 9-inch baking pan. Pour boiling water around the ramekins to about an inch.
5. Bake for 20-25 minutes or until the custard jiggles like jello when you lightly shake the ramekin. Refrigerate for 2 hours for the perfect consistency.

GUT-HEALING KETO
ICE CREAM

This is a delicious low-carb ice cream that doubles as a fantastic gut nourishing recipe due to the presence of the Elemental Diet powder and glutamine. I'm lazy, so I don't use an ice cream maker, though you could if you have one. I just use a big ol' blender.

PEANUT-BUTTER-CHOCOLATE
KETO ICE CREAM

This is another variation of ice cream that uses the same preparation instructions as above, but with different ingredients. After my baseball games when I was a kid, my dad used to take me to Dairy Queen for a giant Reese's Pieces Peanut Butter Cup Blizzard. I consider this to be a nostalgic, far healthier version of that decadent treat, chock-full of amino acids, and healthy fats.

SCREAMIN' SEX
ICE CREAM

Nitric oxide dilates your blood vessels, and acts almost like a "full-body Viagra." After I pondered on all the nitric oxide-inducing ingredients one could have for dessert on a hot date night or before slipping away to the bedroom with one's significant other, I whipped up a batch of this ice cream on a whim and — holy hell — say goodbye to the little blue pill and say hell to screamin' sex! This stuff packs a punch for blood flow for both him and her and is also a fantastic pre-workout blood flow booster too.

Total Time

8 hours 5 minutes

Tools And Materials

Blender

GUT-HEALING KETO ICE CREAM

Ingredients

6 egg yolks

4 scoops Thorne Mediclear SGS (I recommend chocolate flavor) or Dr. Ruscio's Functional Medicine Formulations Elemental Health powder

3g glutamine powder (I use NOW Foods)

3 scoops powdered colostrum

8 droppers-full Omica Organics vanilla or butterscotch toffee stevia

1 teaspoon sea salt

1 can full-fat, organic coconut milk

PEANUT-BUTTER-CHOCOLATE KETO ICE CREAM

Ingredients

5 scoops Ancient Nutrition Peanut Butter Bone Broth Powder

5 scoops Ancient Nutrition Chocolate Collagen Powder

Stevia or monk fruit sweetener to taste

5 egg yolks

1 avocado

2 tablespoons coconut cream

2 tablespoons cinnamon

2 teaspoons sea salt

2 tablespoons almond butter

Ice and bone broth or full-fat, organic coconut milk to desired texture

Instructions

1. Blend on high for 2-3 minutes, until everything is mixed well. Refrigerate overnight for a "pudding" texture or freeze overnight for an "ice-cream" texture.
2. If opting for the frozen version, I like to pull it out of the freezer 30-60 minutes before consuming (e.g. before dinner) to soften.
3. For added calories or flavor, sprinkle with a chopped-up, frozen Kion Clean Energy Bar, cacao nibs, unsweetened coconut flakes, or any other crunchy topping of choice.

SCREAMIN' SEX ICE CREAM

Ingredients

2 cans full-fat, organic coconut milk

2 cups Addictive Wellness raw cacao powder

10 scoops Ancient Nutrition multi collagen powder

5 teaspoons ashwagandha

5 tablespoons Cnidium fruit extract*

10 scoops Organifi red juice

10 dropperfuls Omica Organics butterscotch toffee stevia

10 dropperfuls Essential Oil Wizardry epimedium tincture

10 dropperfuls Essential Oil Wizardry damiana tincture

*Notes

Look up the research on Cnidium fruit extract — this one alone has some pretty interesting sex/libido enhancement and anti-aging properties.

Instructions

1. Blend on high for 2 minutes, then freeze overnight in a rectangular cake pan or stainless steel ice cream container. You could also use all these same ingredients in an ice cream maker.

This stuff is potent, you don't need to eat more than ½ cup for effects!!

ZERO-CARB JAPANESE "JELLY CUBES"

The last time I was in Tokyo, I was absolutely overwhelmed by the variety of novel foods I'd never had a chance to try before, including a fascinating little side dish, served to me at a sushi bar called "tokoroten." Served as bite-sized cubes with the texture of jello, these tiny treats were light, refreshing, incredibly satiating, and oh-so-delicious when dipped in a bit of soy sauce and vinegar that I just had to attempt to re-create them upon my return home.

Tokoroten is technically a traditional Japanese dish made with "jelly noodles." These jelly noodles are agarophytes, which is a seaweed that has been a staple in Japanese cuisine for over a thousand years. It is traditionally made by boiling red algae until it becomes jelly. It can then be eaten in the form of noodles or cubes as a savory dish or as a dessert, depending on what kind of additional spices and ingredients are added. Tokoroten only contains about 2 calories per 100g so it is not only zero-carb, but also extremely low-calorie. But because it contains about 99% water, it will satiate you in a surprisingly effective way. It's also dense in minerals that are wonderful for your thyroid and adrenals, including iodine, molybdenum, and magnesium.

Tokoroten is incredibly easy to make, so long as you have one key ingredient: "Kanten." In Japan, kanten is sold at every supermarket. In other countries, it is often confused with agar-agar, which is another type of seaweed-derived jelly. Problem is, agar-agar isn't firm enough to make a properly textured jelly cube. But it turns out that one of my favorite food companies — Miracle Noodles — makes Kanten noodles shipped in tiny convenient single-serving packages. So here's exactly how I made my jelly cubes using Kanten noodles.

Total Time

7 hours 10 minutes

Ingredients

1 package Miracle noodles Kanten noodles

2 cups water

2 tablespoons Great Lakes gelatin (optional, but adds extra amino acids and firmness)

Instructions

1. In a small saucepan or pot, soak the kanten in the water for about 4 hours. (This is optional, and doesn't have to be done if you're in a hurry, but will improve texture.)

2. Turn the stovetop to low-medium, and heat water as you stir kanten noodles with a fork. After about 10 minutes of heating and frequent stirring, the noodles will "melt" into a goopy texture. At some point during the heating and stirring process, you can add your gelatin if you decide to use it.

3. Pour the final goopy mass into a shallow glass container and refrigerate for 2-3 hours until cubes "set" and become solid.

4. Cut into small, bite-sized squares and enjoy!

Although I suppose these cubes could be classified in a cookbook as a snack or side, I more often turn to them as a sweet treat and a low-carb dessert. For this approach, I drizzle my jelly cubes with a touch of organic honey or molasses and pop them into my mouth with a chopstick, or eat with a spoon served over a bit of vanilla coconut ice cream. However, for a savory side to sushi, salads, or any other lunch or dinner dish, you can also top your jelly cubes with a bit of sea salt or Thomas Cowan's Sea Vegetables Powder, rice vinegar, soy sauce, or miso paste.

SOURDOUGH
CINNAMON ROLLS

It takes great self-control on my part when I wake in the morning to the glorious aroma of my wife Jessa's twist on a cinnamon roll wafting all the way up to the bedroom. These rolls, in addition to containing all the health benefits of sourdough bread, are blessed with a chewy inner texture and a crunchy outer coating that makes each giant roll pure breakfast bliss. Yes, I definitely reserve my own consumption of these rolls for a "higher carb day" treat or a relaxed Sunday breakfast with the family, but it's always worth it. Once you try them, you'll never think of Cinnabon the same way again!

Total Time

First rising time: 8 hours | Second rising time: 2 hours | Prep and baking: 45 minutes

Tools And Materials

9 x 13-inch cake pan

Ingredients For The Rolls

1½ cups active sourdough starter*

2 eggs

1 cup lukewarm water

¼ cup avocado oil

1 teaspoon salt

6 cups of unbleached all-purpose flour

*Notes

Please refer to note re. sourdough starter on page 78.

Instructions For The Rolls

1. Combine the first 5 ingredients into a bowl, and mix well.*
2. Add 4 cups of flour to the bowl and mix. The dough should start holding together, but you should still be able to mix it by hand.
3. Use ½ cup of flour to flour the counter, and pour the dough directly onto the floured counter. Begin to knead the dough. Only add small amounts of more flour if the dough begins to stick to the counter. You are looking for a nice soft dough that holds together.
4. Knead the dough for 10 minutes in a constant movement so it doesn't stick to your countertop.
5. Return the dough to the bowl and cover. Allow the dough to rise for 8 hours or overnight.

*Notes

For a sweet dough, add ¼ cup of organic sucanat to the dough (in step 1).

Ingredients For The Filling

4 tablespoons melted butter

2 tablespoons Ceylon cinnamon (this reduces your blood sugar response to the carbohydrates)

¾ cup organic sucanat (unrefined cane sugar) or for a sugar-free filling, Swerve brown sweetener

Instructions For Filling

1. Melt the butter. Add in the cinnamon and sweetener to the butter, and mix well.
2. Oil a 9 x 13-inch cake pan. Lightly flour the counter, and throw that dough that was rising for 8 hours out onto the floured surface.
3. Roll the dough out to approximately a 16 x 30-inch rectangle. Then, pour the filling on top of the dough.
4. Spread the filling all the way to the edges of the dough. Starting at one end of the 16-inch side of the dough, begin to roll the dough up. Be sure to keep the roll nice and tight.
5. With a serrated knife, mark the middle of the roll then mark the quarters of the roll (this ensures that the rolls remain similar sizes). Make the middle cuts then the quarter cuts, then cut the quarter cuts in half using a gentle sawing motion.
6. Do not press the knife through the dough (you will lose the filling if you do).
7. Arrange the rolls in the pan. Cover, and let the rolls rise for 2 hours.
8. Bake at 350 °F for 30 minutes.

14

COCKTAILS

On June 1st, 2017, Florence Bearse celebrated her 100th birthday, making her one of the very few people who experience a full century of life. When asked what the key to her health was, Florence responded without hesitation.

"I like my wine," she said.

Florence isn't alone. Spanish vineyard owner Antonio Docampo Garcia, who was still overseeing his vineyard at 107 years old, credited daily red wine consumption as the key to his prevailing mental fitness. Same with 108-year-old Eileen Ash, who gave this prescription for staying sharp well into old age: two glasses of red wine every night, plus plenty of yoga.

A lot of centenarians (people who live to be 100) consider wine the key to their extraordinary healthspan. They may be onto something: **moderate daily alcohol consumption** is a cultural staple in almost every single **Blue Zone** — the regions of the world where people live the longest and healthiest (for more on the Blue Zones, check out the comprehensive longevity section in my book *Boundless*, particularly Chapter 21: "Longevity Decoded").

Yet paradoxically, alcohol is also well-established as a brain toxin. A large body of research shows that drinking damages your brain cells and can contribute to dementia, stroke risk, brain inflammation, and more. So, is alcohol healthy or harmful for your brain? Almost all of us have heard both sides. As it turns out, there's a fair amount of nuance when it comes to alcohol and brain health.

First things first: yes, alcohol is a toxin. It can be very dangerous, and can certainly damage your brain, especially when you drink too much of it. Drinking to excess contributes to brain damage in a variety of ways, including induction of **alcohol-induced dementia** and significant brain shrinkage, impaired focus, and memory due to the brain's prefrontal cortex inhibition, **brain inflammation**, and elevated stroke risk. Everyone is different, but most research defines the type of excessive drinking that can cause these types of issues to be 4 or more drinks for men and 3 or more drinks for women.

So yes, most research suggests excess alcohol poses significant health risks. But where does that leave moderate drinking? Roughly defined as 2-3 glasses of wine a night for men and 1-2 glasses for women, moderate alcohol consumption may actually improve brain health in a few different ways, including:

Better longevity and decreased cognitive decline: People who have 1-3 glasses of alcohol a day are **three times more likely than non-drinkers** to live to age 85. Daily moderate drinkers are also twice as likely to be cognitively healthy at 85 — non-drinkers and heavy drinkers are much more likely to develop dementia or Alzheimer's. Other studies have also concluded that drinking in moderation protects against cognitive decline. Red wine, in particular, contains **antioxidants that decrease your risk of dementia.**

Better waste clearance: Mice given small amounts of alcohol (equivalent to a couple of drinks a day) showed an **increase in glymphatic function** — their brain's ability to clear waste products. Your glymphatic system clears out inflammatory waste and gets rid of the damaged proteins that contribute to Alzheimer's, Parkinson's, and other forms of dementia. Improved toxin clearance could explain why moderate daily drinkers are twice as likely as non-drinkers to be cognitively healthy at 85.

Decreased stroke risk: A study of 5,400 people found that those who had 2-3 drinks a day (1-2 drinks a day for women) were **significantly less likely to have a stroke** than non-drinkers were.

Lower inflammation: Moderate alcohol consumption **decreases inflammation**, including brain inflammation. **Wine is especially good for your brain**, thanks to its rich variety of anti-inflammatory polyphenols and antioxidants.

Stress relief: Moderate drinking **relieves mental stress** and normalizes your cortisol (stress hormone) response after a psychologically stressful experience. You don't want to become dependent on alcohol to manage your stress, of course, but a glass or two of wine can turn off your stress response and help you relax at the end of a long day.

As a matter of fact, four of the Blue Zones engage in moderate and regular alcohol consumption, which most likely **contributes** to their robust mental health and overall longevity. Take the Sardinians, for example. They are famous for their regular consumption of a regional red wine called "Cannonau," a type of dry wine that contains **2-3 times the flavonoid content of other wines**. Not familiar with the term "Cannonau"? It's actually known elsewhere and more popularly as Grenache!

Consuming wine with or before a meal can assist the body with the absorption of the artery-scrubbing flavonoid antioxidants in the wine, and studies have shown that consumption of wine as part of a Mediterranean diet can reduce the risk of cardiovascular disease and cancers. Regular low-level physical activity boosts these benefits even more. According to a study in the European Society of Cardiology, moderate wine drinking combined with regular physical activity is a potent combination for cardiovascular disease prevention. As a matter of fact, Sardinian shepherds often walk up to 5 miles a day to tend to their flocks — and often carry along a lunch of unleavened bread, fava beans, Pecorino cheese, and a local Cannonau wine.

You're no doubt also familiar with resveratrol, a polyphenol found in the skin of grapes that may **protect the body** against oxidative damage that places it at higher risk for cancer, heart disease, and dementia, and can also combat the formation of plaque found in the brains of dementia patients. This may also be why **weekly consumption of alcohol is also associated with better cognitive function in old age**. Plenty of additional research backs up the link between wine intake, low stress, and longevity.

This type of frequent, moderate alcohol consumption is one of my own nightly habits — most often accomplished via a digestif and bitters rich Moscow Mule (usually made with Zevia sugar-free ginger beer), a shot of gin or vodka over ice with a squeeze of lemon, and a generous portion of bitters (a drink I affectionately call "Ben & Jitters"), or an organic, biodynamic glass of red wine from a company such as Dry Farm Wines. If I'm out and about, most bars can fashion a variant of any of the cocktails I've just mentioned, and most wines I'll order from Italy, France, or New Zealand, even if not labeled organic, are typically prepared using more old-world organic or biodynamic wine preparation methods.

As a matter of fact, I have one drink just about every night, very rarely have two or more drinks, and — since I began this practice six years ago — have never once been drunk or experienced a hangover. So now that you're convinced you may not need to swear off alcohol altogether, let's dive into a few of my favorite evening cocktail recipes:

For all resources, books, tools, and ingredients mentioned throughout this chapter go to:
BoundlessCookbook.com/cocktails

BEN &
JITTERS

This is one of my favorite cocktails to order because just about any bar can make it. I simply request a selection of house bitters over ice with a squeeze of lemon, a splash of apple cider vinegar (if they have it), and a shot of clean-burning alcohol, such as vodka, mezcal, or — you guessed it, and as the name of this drink implies — gin. Get it? Ben and Jitters? This is an easy one to make at home as well if you have good bitters.

Two of my favorites are Ebo Lebo (a more difficult one that you'll often have to order from Italy) or Urban Moonshine bitters. Kin Euphorics and Essential Oil Wizardry also have some interesting bitters and blends that can be used to spice up your cocktails. I'm not particularly attentive to exact measurements or ratios when whipping up most of my cocktails and instead just use a "bit of this and bit of that" approach, although, for the alcohol itself, I'm always careful not to exceed more than 1.5 ounces (about the equivalent of a shot glass).

ELDERBERRY JUICE AND ORGANIC WINE OVER ICE

Some might consider this to be a bastardization of a good glass of organic wine, but I quite enjoy it, especially due to the added vitamin C and immune-boosting benefits of the elderberry. I simply pour a glass of organic, biodynamic red wine over ice and then stir in about a teaspoon of elderberry juice concentrate or a shot of elderberry juice (there are a variety of elderberry options on both Amazon and Thrive Market). This refreshing drink is also quite good as a summertime sangria if you substitute frozen organic cherries or blueberries for the ice!

Total Time

5 minutes

Ingredients

12 ounces organic, biodynamic red wine

1 teaspoon Elderberry juice concentrate

1 cup of ice

Instructions

1. Pour 12 ounces of organic, biodynamic red wine over ice.
2. Stir in about a teaspoon of elderberry juice concentrate.
3. Enjoy immediately!

MOSCOW MULE
WITH
ZEVIA GINGER BEER

In college, my drink of choice was a Moscow Mule, provided it was served in the traditional copper mug (nothing less). Problem is, most ginger beer is chock-full of high fructose corn syrup. But I discovered a stevia-flavored ginger beer that has once again allowed me to enjoy a good mule. The same company that makes the ginger beer (Zevia) also makes a very good tonic water that can be used for variants of any cocktail recipe.

Total Time

10 minutes

Ingredients

3 mint leaves

A shot of vodka or gin (for a Mexican Mule, I'll sometimes use tequila)

Juice from ½ lime

4-6 ounces Zevia Ginger Beer

Extra lime and mint for garnish

Instruction

1. Muddle the mint in the bottom of a glass with the alcohol and lime juice.
2. Add in ice and top off with Zevia Ginger Beer Mixer.
3. Garnish with extra mint and a slice of lime, and enjoy!

15

RESOURCES

For all resources, books, tools, and ingredients mentioned throughout this book go to BoundlessCookbook.com/resources

BOOKS

Anti-Factory Farm by Evgeny Trufkin

Boundless by Ben Greenfield

Don't Waste Your Life by John Piper

Eating on the Wild Side by Jo Robinson

Folks, This Ain't Normal by Joel Salatin

Grain Brain by David Perlmutter

Health for Godly Generations by Renée DeGroot

Living by Design by Ray Strand and Bill Ewing

Regenerate by Sayer Ji

Sourdough: Recipes for Rustic Fermented Breads, Sweets, Savories, and More by Sarah Owen

Stress Less, Accomplish More by Emily Fletcher

The Art of Fermentation by Sandor Katz

The Blue Zones by Dan Buettner

The Carnivore Code by Paul Saladino, MD

The Human Photosynthesis by Arturo Solis Herrera MD, Ph.D.

The Immunity Code by Joel Greene

The Marvelous Pigness of Pigs by Joel Salatin

The Plant Paradox by Dr. Stephen Gundry

The Sprouts Book by Doug Evans

Undoctored by William Davis, MD

Wildatarian by Teri Cochrane

KITCHEN TOOLS, MATERIALS, AND EQUIPMENT

Braising Pan

Breville Joule Sous Vide

Cheesecake Mold Pan

Clay Pot For Sourdough Bread

Essential Oils

Food Dehydrator

Hydrogen Peroxide — Food Grade

Meat Thermometer

Musubi Maker

Pastry Knife

Proofing Box

Sprouting Jar

Sprouter Without A Stand

Stasher 100% Silicone Reusable Food Bags

Traeger Grill

MEAT, FISH, AND CHICKEN

Meat

American Grassfed Association - AmericanGrassfed.org

BelCampo Meats - BelCampo.com

Eat Wild - EatWild.com

Fossil Farms - FossilFarms.com

5 Bar Beef - 5BarBeef.com

Piedmontese - Piedmontese.com

Thrive Market - ThriveMarket.com

US Wellness Meats - GrassLandBeef.com

White Oak Pastures - WhiteOakPastures.com

Wild Idea Buffalo Company - WildIdeaBuffalo.com

The Spruce Eats - TheSpruceEats.com

Fish

Vital Choice Wild Red Alaskan Sockeye Salmon

Wild Planet Wild Pink Salmon

Wild-Caught Salmon

Seatopia

Chicken

Eggs - CornuCopia.org or EatWild.com

PANTRY ITEMS

Acacia Fiber

Addictive Wellness Raw Cacao Powder

Almond Wraps

Blueberry Powder

Broccoli And Friends Seed Mix

Cacao Extract

Cacao Nibs

Celtic Salt

Coconut Milk

Coconut Sugar

Colima Sea Salt

Dr. Cowan's Garden Low Oxalate Greens

Dr. Cowan's Garden Sea Vegetable Powder

Dry Farm Wines

Elderberry Juice

Einkorn Flour

Emerald Cove Organic Pacific Nori

Great Lakes Powdered Gelatin

Hawaiian Black Lava Sea Salt, Coarse Grain

Hawaiian Black Lava Sea Salt, Fine Grain

Hawaiian Black Lava Sea Salt, Unrefined

Kefir Grains

Kettle & Fire

Kion Clean Energy Bar

King Arthur Organic Unbleached All-Purpose Flour

Kona Black Salt

MCT Oil

MiCacao

Miracle Noodles

Molina Grassi USDA Organic Italian Flour

NOW Foods Desiccated Liver Powder

Nut Butter

Omica Organics

Omica Organics Vanilla or Butterscotch Toffee Stevia

Organic Unrefined Sugar — Sucanat

Primal Kitchen Aioli Mayo

Primal Kitchen Tartar Sauce

Primal Palate Pumpkin Spice

Sourdough Starter

Swerve Sweetener

Sunflower Lecithin

Tapioca Starch

Zevia Sugar-Free Ginger Beer

SUPPLEMENTS

Ancient Nutrition Chocolate Collagen Powder

Ancient Nutrition Multi Collagen Powder

Ancient Nutrition Peanut Butter Bone Broth Powder

Ashwagandha

BioGaia Gastrus L-Reuteri Probiotic Capsules

Chamomile Powder

Cnidium Fruit Extract

Colostrum

Colostrum Powder

Creatine Powder

Elemental Diet Powder

Elemental Heal Formula

Essential Oil Wizardry Damiana Tincture

Essential Oil Wizardry Epimedium Tincture

Four Sigmatic Chaga Mushroom Extract

Four Sigmatic Cordyceps Mushroom Extract

Four Sigmatic Lion's Mane

Four Sigmatic Reishi

Four Sigmatic Ten Mushrooms Blend

Glutamine

Glycine Powder

Hca/Garcinia Powder

Immortalis Klotho Formula

Lakanto Monk Fruit Sweetener

Organifi Red Juice

Pau D'Arco Powdered Tea

Prebiotic Powder

Quercetin Powder

Resveratrol

Thomas Cowan's Vegetable Powders

Thorne AM/PM

Thorne Mediclear SGS

WEBSITES

FeastingAtHome.com

Go Greenfields podcast - GoGreenfields.com

Himalayan Tartary Buckwheat

BigBoldHealth.com/news/the-story-of-big-bold-health/

Or watch on YouTube Himalayan Tartary Buckwheat: Meet the Next Superfood! | Big Bold Health Podcast Episode 20

Seafood Watch - SeafoodWatch.org

16

REFERENCES

Bickford PC; Tan J; Shytle RD; Sanberg CD; El-Badri N; Sanberg PR; Nutraceuticals Synergistically Promote Proliferation of Human Stem Cells. Stem cells and development.

Brust, J.C.M., 2010. Ethanol and cognition: Indirect effects, neurotoxicity, and neuroprotection: A review. International journal of environmental research and public health. Available at: https://www.ncbi.nlm.nih.gov/pmc/articles/PMC2872345/.

Caruana, M., Cauchi, R. & amp; Vassallo, N., 2016. Putative Role of Red Wine Polyphenols against Brain Pathology in Alzheimer's and Parkinson's Disease. Frontiers in nutrition. Available at: https://www.ncbi.nlm.nih.gov/pmc/articles/PMC4981604/.

Grønbaek, M. et al., 2000. Type of alcohol consumed and mortality from all causes, coronary heart disease, and cancer. Annals of internal medicine. Available at: https://www.ncbi.nlm.nih.gov/pubmed/10975958/).

Gupta, S. & amp; Warner, J., 2008. Alcohol-related dementia: A 21st-century silent epidemic? The British journal of psychiatry: The journal of mental science. Available at: https://www.ncbi.nlm.nih.gov/pubmed/18978310.

Hamblin, J., 2014. Wine and Exercise: A Promising Combination. The Atlantic. Available at: https://www.theatlantic.com/health/archive/2014/09/working-with-the-wine-not-against-it/379504/.

Lee, S.J. et al., 2015. Moderate alcohol intake reduces risk of ischemic stroke in Korea. Neurology. Available at: https://www.ncbi.nlm.nih.gov/pmc/articles/PMC4664129/.

Lundgaard, I. et al., 2018. Beneficial effects of low alcohol exposure, but adverse effects of high alcohol intake on glymphatic function. Nature News. Available at: https://www.nature.com/articles/s41598-018-20424-y.

Marambaud, P., Zhao, H. & amp; Davies, P., 2005. Resveratrol promotes clearance of Alzheimer's disease amyloid-beta peptides. The Journal of biological chemistry. Available at: https://www.ncbi.nlm.nih.gov/pubmed/16162502.

Ogden Publications, I., Meet Real Free-Range Eggs. Mother Earth News. Available at: https://www.motherearthnews.com/real-food/free-range-eggs-zmaz07onzgoe.

Anon, 2020. Power 9®. Blue Zones. Available at: https://www.bluezones.com/2016/11/power-9/.

Reas, E.T. et al., 2016. Moderate, regular alcohol consumption is associated with higher cognitive function in older community-dwelling adults. Journal of Prevention of Alzheimer's Disease. Available at: http://www.jpreventionalzheimer.com/all-issues.html?article=178

Richard, E.L. et al., 2017. Alcohol Intake and Cognitively Healthy Longevity in Community-Dwelling Adults: The Rancho Bernardo Study. Journal of Alzheimer's disease: JAD. Available at: https://www.ncbi.nlm.nih.gov/pmc/articles/PMC5939941/.

Ros, E. et al., 2014. Mediterranean Diet and Cardiovascular Health: Teachings of the PREDIMED Study. OUP Academic. Available at: http://advances.nutrition.org/content/5/3/330S.full.

Roux, A. et al., 2014. Chronic Ethanol Consumption Profoundly Alters Regional Brain Ceramide and Sphingomyelin Content in Rodents. ACS Chemical Neuroscience, 6(2), pp.247–259.

Schrieks, I.C. et al., 2016. Moderate alcohol consumption after a mental stressor attenuates the endocrine stress response. Alcohol (Fayetteville, N.Y.). Available at: https://www.ncbi.nlm.nih.gov/pubmed/27916140.

Simonetti, P., Pietta, P. & amp; Testolin, G., 1997. Polyphenol Content and Total Antioxidant Potential of Selected Italian Wines. Journal of Agricultural and Food Chemistry, 45(4), pp.1152–1155.

Wang, J.J. et al., 2008. Effects of moderate alcohol consumption on inflammatory biomarkers. Acta cardiologica. Available at: https://www.ncbi.nlm.nih.gov/pubmed/18372583.

17

ABOUT THE AUTHOR

Ben Greenfield is a human performance consultant, speaker, and *New York Times* bestselling author of 13 books, including the wildly popular titles *Beyond Training* (BeyondTrainingBook.com), *Boundless* (BoundlessBook.com), and *Fit Soul* (FitSoulBook. com).

As a former collegiate tennis, water polo, and volleyball player, bodybuilder, 13-time Ironman triathlete, and professional obstacle course racer, Ben has been voted by the NSCA as America's top personal trainer and by Greatist as one of the top 100 Most Influential People In Health and Fitness.

A frequent contributor to health and wellness publications and websites and a highly sought after speaker, Ben's understanding of functional exercise, nutrition, and the delicate balance between performance and health has helped thousands of people around the world achieve their goals and improve their quality of life — from high-level CEO's to soccer moms to professional athletes and beyond.

Ben is an advisor, investor, and board member of multiple corporations in the health and fitness industry, and is also the co-founder of **KION** (GetKion.com), a nutritional supplements company that combines time-honored superfoods with modern science to allow human beings to achieve peak performance, defy aging, and live an adventurous, fulfilling, joyful, and limitless life.

Via online, phone, e-mail, and in-person consulting, Ben coaches and trains individuals (BenGreenfieldCoaching.com) all over the world for health, longevity, and performance. He also works with individuals, corporations, and teams for body and brain performance enhancement, and specializes in performance, fat loss, digestion, brain, sleep, hormone, anti-aging, parenting, relationships, smart drugs, nootropics, and overall wellness for achieving an optimized life.

Ben lives in Spokane, Washington, with his wife, Jessa, and twin boys, River and Terran, where he enjoys worshiping God and praising Christ, swinging kettlebells, fiction, guitar, ukulele, spearfishing, bowhunting, plant foraging, and cooking.

CREDENTIALS

- Bachelor's and master's degrees from the University of Idaho in sports science and exercise physiology.
- Personal training, strength, and conditioning certifications from the National Strength and Conditioning Association (NSCA).
- Sports nutrition certification from the International Society of Sports Nutrition (ISSN).
- Advanced bicycle fitting certification from Serotta, the "Harvard" of bicycle fitting schools.
- Spartan SGX coaching certification.
- Over 20 years of experience in coaching professional, collegiate, and recreational athletes from all sports.

Ben hosts the highly popular fitness, nutrition, and wellness website BenGreenfieldFitness.com, a site with over a million monthly visitors, featuring articles, podcasts, and product reviews from Ben.

In addition to multiple daytime and reality TV show competitions, Ben has also appeared in and been a contributor to *Forbes*, *Men's Health*, *Huffington Post*, Fox News, *Triathlete* magazine, *LAVA* magazine, Endurance Planet, and has been featured in WebMD, *Prevention* magazine, *Shape* magazine, *Men's Health*, *Men's Fitness*, *Women's Running* magazine, *Inside Triathlon*, NBC, Fox, Entheos Academy, CreativeLIVE, MindBodyGreen, Udemy, Veria Live TV, CBS Sports, MindValley University, *Outside Magazine*, and beyond.

As a **public speaker on longevity, anti-aging, biohacking, fitness, nutrition, and cognition** (BenGreenfieldSpeaking.com), Ben has hosted several top-ranked fitness and health podcasts on iTunes, including the Ben Greenfield Fitness (BenGreenfieldFitness.com) show, Endurance Planet, Get-Fit Guy, and Obstacle Dominator. Ben speaks around the world and, in addition to presenting multi-day conferences in global hotspots such as Sweden, Finland, Dubai, London, and Thailand, he has been a keynote lecturer at private financial and corporate events, the Hawaii Ironman World Championships Medical Conference, Biohacker's Summits, PaleoFX, MindValley, American Academy of Anti-Aging Medicine, Academy of Regenerative Practices, CalJam, FitCon, Tedx, The Ancestral Health Symposium, Runga, and numerous other private health retreats.

18

FINAL WORDS

Do you know the most exasperating part about writing a cookbook? Really, it's the same conundrum I experience when writing anything — just about the time I think I've said everything I want to say, I learn something new and interesting that I wish I would've included in the book!

Allow me to illustrate a few examples for you. Upon putting the finishing touches on the *Boundless Cookbook*, I found myself even more excited about cooking than ever, and so, one day, while tooling around the kitchen, I eyed a large bag of grass-fed, grass-finished beef liver in my refrigerator and thought... *I wonder what liver jerky tastes like?*

I can't believe I'd never thought of making liver jerky before. So, I set about to create. I grabbed the bag of liver and soaked it for 24 hours in kefir (yep, the same kefir you find a recipe for on page 125). Turns out kefir is one of the best soaking mediums to tenderize meats and organs and to particularly remove the "gaminess" flavor from any wild meat or organs. I then rinsed and thin-sliced the soaked liver, then liberally coated it with Primal Kitchen BBQ Sauce, salt and — don't laugh — a thick coating of Organifi Red Juice, theorizing that this final addition to my coating would add a sweet, caramelizing quality to my jerky, along with a blast of berry flavor and a big boost of nitric oxide and other blood-building compounds. The final step was simple: I dehydrated the jerky in my Excalibur Food Dehydrator at 155 degrees for 12 hours...and - voila! This tasty snack turned out to have addictively superior flavor, amped-up nutrient density, and a perfect texture combination of satiating chewiness and slight, savory, sweet moistness. I've since successfully repeated this experiment with another wonderful, nutrient-dense organ meat: heart.

Since writing this cookbook, I've also discovered the magic of a pressure cooker. A pressure cooker is simply a sealed pot with a valve that controls the steam pressure inside. As the pot heats, the liquid inside forms steam, which raises the pressure in the pot. This high pressure steam raises the boiling point of any liquid in the pot, which helps the food to cook faster, and promotes caramelization and browning in a way that creates surprisingly deep and complex flavor profiles of even the most difficult-to-cook or traditionally "tough" cuts of meat, such as stew meat or chuck roast. It also works as a convenient time hack for quickly preparing dishes such as rice or spaghetti squash — in as little as eight minutes! So over the past few weeks, I've used a Power XL Pressure Cooker to prepare a giant pork loin, two enormous spaghetti squashes, and melt-in-your-mouth short ribs, the latter of which was amplified to pure perfection by accompanying it in the pressure cooker with equal parts bone broth and red wine, along with a splash of apple cider vinegar and hot sauce.

I've also discovered convenient methods for using tools you've already discovered within the pages of the *Boundless Cookbook*. Take sous vide, for example. It turns out that to make the crispiest, most evenly-cooked pork belly (see recipe page 48) you'll ever taste, you can simply wake up in the morning, take a big ol' slab of uncured bacon, drop it in a sous bag with a bit of olive oil, rosemary, and thyme, put the water at 165 °F, then simply walk away for 8-12 hours. For dinner, you remove the pork belly from the sous vide bag, slice it as thick or thin as you please, and then give it a quick sear for 1-2 minutes per side on a skillet. You'll thank me forever after experiencing pork belly prepared this way!

Then there's gravy. For years, I've been adding cornstarch to my leftover sauces to make a thick dipping gravy, but I've recently discovered that the arguably healthier options of either arrowroot flour or tapioca flour works just as well to thicken sauces and gravies, as does simply tossing a handful of butter-fried mushrooms into your liquid. And there's yet another feather to add to the cap of my cooking skills that I can now rely upon the rest of my culinary life!

Finally, as you've no doubt suspected if you've read this entire cookbook, I'm a huge fan of nutrient-dense superfoods, such as the sprouts you can read about on page 93. I'll often freeze my sprouts to concentrate the cancer-fighting compounds such as sulforaphane, then toss a handful of this plant kingdom superfood into my morning smoothie. But now I accompany my frozen sprouts with another superfood from the animal kingdom: liver. It turns out that it's quite simple to puree raw liver in a blender, pour it into silicone molds, then freeze. The result are tiny frozen liver "bites" that you can toss into any smoothie, thus masking the organ meat flavor (if that's something you don't like), while simultaneously boosting the nutrient content of your smoothie through the roof!

Other new, nutrient-dense ingredients I've been experimenting with include "kaniwa", an ancient supergrain relative of quinoa that also shares many of quinoa's healthy attributes like fiber, iron, calcium, and protein, but doesn't contain quinoa's bitter outer coating of saponin; "lucuma", a tropical fruit extract native to South America that serves as an incredibly flavorful, low-glycemic sweetener; and "asafoetida", a traditional south Indian spice made from the dried resin of a tree with a pungent and funky flavor that can infuse any dish with a unique meaty, savory essence.

It may seem intimidating to you to know that there exists all these new and different cooking methods and ingredients you've perhaps never heard of. But that's the magic of cooking, and life in general, isn't it? It's a constant discovering and learning process that — for the curious lover-of-life — makes each new day that much more refreshing and invigorating.

Based on that concept, I now challenge you to venture beyond the pages of the *Boundless Cookbook* and continue to discover and learn new tips, tricks, tactics, and tools to enhance your culinary experience. Find a fringe ingredient (maybe even something growing in your backyard!) and play with it in your next cooking project. Go visit an ethnic restaurant, and take a few menu photos for ideas on a few imaginative recipe twists for your next kitchen experiment. Watch a couple episodes or even an entire season of a cooking competition show for fresh inspiration and ideas. You get the idea: cooking is a never-ending process of magical discovery that — if you embrace the mystery, intrigue, and occasional blunder — keeps life stimulating and exciting. I encourage you to enjoy the *Boundless* adventure, and I'll continue to do the same!